THE STORY OF THE
GEMS
A Popular Handbook

AN ANCIENT CRAFT

Stone cutting, the art of the lapidary, was brought to a high
degree of perfection during the time of the Italian Renaissance.

THE STORY OF THE
GEMS
A Popular Handbook

by Herbert P. Whitlock

Curator of Minerals and Gems,
American Museum of Natural History

DOVER PUBLICATIONS, INC.
Mineola, New York

Published in Canada by General Publishing Company, Ltd., 30 Lesmill Road, Don Mills, Toronto, Ontario.
Published in the United Kingdom by Constable and Company, Ltd., 3 The Lanchesters, 162–164 Fulham Palace Road, London W6 9ER.

Bibliographical Note

This Dover edition, first published in 1997, is an unabridged republication of the volume first published by Emerson Books, Inc., New York, in 1942. Two colored plates depicting gems have been relocated to the front and back covers of this edition.

Library of Congress Cataloging-in-Publication Data

Whitlock, Herbert P.
    The story of the gems : a popular handbook / by Herbert P. Whitlock.
        p. cm.
    Previously published: New York : Emerson Books, 1942.
    Includes bibliographical references and index.
    ISBN 0-486-29938-4 (pbk.)
    1. Precious stones.   2. Glyptics.   I. Title.
QE392.W5   1997
553.8–dc21   97–36343
                                                                        CIP

Manufactured in the United States of America
Dover Publications, Inc., 31 East 2nd Street, Mineola, N.Y. 11501

TO
LUCRETIA PERRY OSBORN
TO WHOSE INSIGHT, TASTE AND
ENTHUSIASM
THE PRESENT INSTALLATION
OF THE
MORGAN GEM COLLECTION
OWES VERY MUCH OF
ITS ATTRACTIVENESS
THIS LITTLE BOOK IS APPRECIATIVELY
DEDICATED

Contents

FOREWORD . . . . *Page* xiii

INTRODUCTION . . . . *Chapter* I. *Page* 3

THE ANTIQUE USE OF GEMS . . . *Chapter* II. *Page* 15

THE ART OF THE LAPIDARY . . . . *Chapter* III. *Page* 25

THE FORMS IN WHICH GEMS ARE CUT *Chapter* IV. *Page* 43

THE DIAMOND . . . . *Chapter* V. *Page* 67

FAMOUS DIAMONDS OF THE WORLD . *Chapter* VI. *Page* 77

PRECIOUS STONES OTHER THAN
    DIAMONDS . . . . *Chapter* VII. *Page* 89

THE SEMIPRECIOUS STONES . . . . *Chapter* VIII. *Page* 101

SEMIPRECIOUS STONES (*Continued*) . . *Chapter* IX. *Page* 113

CHRYSOBERYL AND OPAL . . . . *Chapter* X. *Page* 123

THE QUARTZ GEMS . . . . . . *Chapter* XI. *Page* 131

THE QUARTZ GEMS (*Continued*) . . . *Chapter* XII. *Page* 141

THE OPAQUE GEMS AND ORNA-
    MENTAL STONES . . . . *Chapter* XIII. *Page* 151

OPAQUE AND ORNAMENTAL STONES *Chapter* XIV. *Page* 163

UNUSUAL GEM STONES . . . . . *Chapter* XV. *Page* 171

ORGANIC PRODUCTS USED AS GEMS . *Chapter* XVI. *Page* 181

LIST OF BOOKS ON GEMS . . . . *Page* 189

DESCRIPTIVE TABLE OF GEMS . . . . *Page* 195

INDEX . . . . *Page* 203

Foreword

A MUSEUM curator has occasion to come in contact with, and to test the reactions of, a great many people, representing a considerable cross section of that complex group known as "the public." In the course of about thirty years of such contacts the writer has come to recognize that people in general can be aroused to an interest in gems when even the most well directed effort to gain a hearing on the subject of the minerals from which the gems originate will appeal at best to only a scattered few.

A course of popular lectures on gems which frankly admitted the public's point of view has been very largely contributory to the preparation of this book.

Some of the matter which went into it has had its initial appearance elsewhere, as, for example, the chapter on the forms in which gems are cut, which was rearranged from a series of articles that appeared in the Jewelers' Circular as long ago as 1917-18, and which are now out of print.

All of the illustrations are from gems and carved objects exhibited in the Morgan Collection of Gems, in the Morgan Hall of the American Museum of Natural History.

The color frontispiece was reproduced from drawings by Katharine Burton Brimer.

The thanks of the writer are extended to the late Mr. T. Edgar Willson, Editor of the Jewelers' Circular, as well as to Mr. Meyer D. Rothschild and Mr. Stephen Varni, for advice regarding the jeweler's viewpoint in relation to matters treated in it.

The writer is also much indebted to Mr. John de Cock, skilled diamond polisher, who posed for the photographs of diamond cleaving, "bruting" and polishing. Also to Mr. Julius Kirschner, photographic artist, for the splendid photographs from which the half-tone illustrations used throughout the text were made.

CHAPTER I

"*Any one that wanted things*
  Touched the jewel and they came,
  We were wealthier than kings
  Could we only do the same."
                    —ALFRED NOYES

CHAPTER I

Introduction

THE minerals that constitute the material out of which our earth is made are used by us in various ways. We make use of the mixture of minerals that we call granite to build our houses, churches and stores.

Out of other minerals we separate the metals without which our so-called civilization would go out of existence like the flame of an extinguished match. How long would our culture last without gold and silver for our money; or iron for our machines and railways, steamers and motors; or copper for the transmission of our telephone current?

And certain of these minerals, only a few of the many hundreds of different kinds of them, we use in their natural state because they appeal to our sense of beauty. These are the gem stones or gem minerals out of which man has fashioned ornaments for his person since long before history began. As he discovered more kinds of minerals, he has added some of these to the category of the gem stones, but, for the most part, the gems whose names are familiar to us have been known and used since very early times.

The relation of minerals to gems is not always an easy one for the layman to grasp. If every different kind of mineral furnished a kind of gem, there would be over one thousand different varieties for the jeweler to remember. In point of fact, only four percent of the mineral species known to science are suitable for the fashioning of gems. Moreover, in very many instances, only certain varieties of a particular mineral answer to the requirements of a gem stone.

Let us then consider briefly the qualifications which combine to confer nobility, as it were, on the members of the mineral family, because in most cases our most beautiful and precious gems are only distinguished varieties of very common and unassuming minerals.

In the first place, the most obvious quality that a gem should possess is beauty of color. From the rich brilliant red of the ruby through the delicate and subtle shades of tourmaline and chrysoberyl, beauty of color is the source of the appeal exercised by these fragments of Mother Earth.

Linked to beauty of color is a second quality which in most cases determines whether or not a mineral will qualify as a gem. A certain degree of transparency, which permits the color qualities of a gem to be developed by the cutting and polishing of the stone, is necessary in most gem minerals.

Again, in order to preserve its transparency and polish against the wear to which a stone worn as jewelry is inevitably subjected, a gem mineral should possess a certain degree of hardness. This requirement is particularly rigid of application to stones which are intended to be mounted in rings, since it is these that are subject to the most strenuous wear.

And lastly, the desirability of a gem is very largely governed by its rarity. We have ample illustration of this point in the single case of the artificially produced sapphires and rubies, which, although possessing all the qualities of the choicest natural gems (beauty of color, hardness, brilliancy), are, on account of the ease with which they are obtained and their attendant low price, little esteemed among the wearers of gems. Nor does the comparatively low price of these artificial members of the royal family among gems in any way affect that of the natural rubies and sapphires. Gem purchasers are willing to pay many times the value of a synthetic gem solely for the rarity of the same gem from a natural source.

To sum up the qualifications which determine whether a certain mineral or a special variety of a mineral will furnish material for gem stones, we have:—

1. Beauty of color.
2. In most instances, transparency.
3. A certain degree of hardness.
4. Rarity of occurrence under these conditions.

The question of color is one that leads to much confusion in our preconceived ideas about gem stones. The popular color of a gem mineral is very apt to dominate our ideas about it to the exclusion of other colors which are often no less attractive. A notable instance of this is to be found in the blue gem variety of the mineral corundum, known as sapphire. Because blue sapphires are so well known and so much sought after, we are, generally speaking, unaware that yellow, violet, green and orange gems are also furnished by the same mineral that provides us with blue sapphires and are known as *fancy sapphires*. So we come to the knowledge that all sapphires are not blue; an astonishing statement to most of us.

Looking at this question of color from another angle, we are very prone to ascribe all gems of a certain color to one particular kind. The preceding paragraph has prepared us for the statement that all topazes are not yellow. In reality they are also light blue, orange, pink and white, but it seems hard for us to believe that all yellow gems are not topazes. This, however, is true in such a measure that, in such a comprehensive assemblage of gems as the Morgan Collection, we can find yellow examples among the corundum gems, the beryl gems, zircons, chrysoberyls, the quartz gems, the feldspar gems, as well as several of those more unusual gem minerals that are seldom met with among cut stones. And what is true of the yellow gems may be stated with equal truth with regard to those of other colors, for we find many kinds of blue gems, of green gems, and of red, purple and colorless gems, until it would seem almost impossible for one to tell, by the eye alone, in what mineral species to place a questionable example. It is true that the experienced expert has, through the constant handling of many examples of different gems, become conscious of very subtle differences of shade which he has learned to associate with the different gem-producing minerals that furnish stones of a certain color. Thus yellow zircons differ slightly in shade from yellow sapphires and yellow chrysoberyls. But even the trained expert is often forced to employ other means of determination than color to aid him in distinguishing some of these gems.

Of course if every cut gem that came under our notice were to be accompanied by some of the rough material from which it was fashioned, the task of determining its mineral source would be relatively easy, because certain characteristics, such as the shape of its crystals, its cleavage and possibly its association with other minerals, would then be more or less apparent. But since all of these aids to the recognition of a mineral are necessarily eliminated when it is cut into the form of a gem, we must seek other and less obvious distinctions in order to recognize different minerals when fashioned as gem stones. Again, many of the tests which are ordinarily used to distinguish mineral species, such as the degree of hardness and the various chemical reactions that determine chemical composition, are not applicable to the testing of a gem stone because they would tend to damage the cutting and fine polish which constitute no small part of its value. It is true that very judicious use is sometimes made of the quality of hardness by using the inconspicuous edge of a cut stone, known as the girdle, as an abrading edge against a known scale of hardness; but even this test must be used with great care and discretion, and is not generally to be recommended.

There are, however, several physical properties common to gem minerals that can be used with perfect safety on cut gems. Some of these are so simple and easily available to those who deal with gems that we will devote a little space to describing them briefly.

Perhaps the most useful of all the physical properties of minerals from the point of view of the gem dealer as an aid to his identification of a questionable gem is its relative weight compared with the weight of an equal volume of pure water. Most of us will remember that this was the test that enabled Archimedes on a certain historic occasion to decide whether his sovereign's crown was made of pure gold or of a baser metal. It is possible for us in this age of progress to determine this relative weight, which we call *specific gravity*, with great ease and accuracy, and to apply it to the identification of gems, to which use this property lends itself most favorably, since gems are for the most part very homogeneous fragments of minerals which have constant and definite relative weights.

Two standard methods for determining the specific gravity of a gem may be used where an accurate balance, such as jewelers use, is available. Either the weight of the stone suspended in water may be used to calculate its relative weight, or the weight of the water displaced by the submerged stone may be found by means of a small specially constructed flask or bottle. The former of these is best adapted to large stones, and the latter to stones of five carats or less.

In the first case, a fine wire, one end of which terminates in a little spiral basket, and the other end in a loop with which to attach it to the hook which carries the weighing pan of the balance, is used for the weighing in water. This wire should be of such a length as to give three or four inches of clearance between the basket and the weighing pan. Water is placed in a convenient glass or beaker supported on a small wooden bench whose height is just sufficient to allow the balance pan to swing freely below it. Of course, neither the bench nor the glass of water should touch the balance pan or its suspending wires. The stone whose relative weight we wish to determine weighs less in water than in air, and this difference in weight exactly equals the weight of the amount of water it displaces. So that in order to determine its relative weight, we have only to compare the gem's weight in air with its loss of weight in water, since water is our unit of comparison for relative weight. With the empty wire basket, and an inch or more of the wire that carries it, entirely submerged in the water, the weight is taken and set aside as a constant which must be used in the calculation whenever this device is used. Let us call this weight C. Then the weight of the stone, taken in the balance pan, the balance being free from the wire basket, we will call A. If now we place the stone in the wire basket and weigh it in water, calling this weighing B, we will have for our determination of its specific gravity (G):—

$$G = \frac{A}{A-(B-C)}$$

Throughout all the weighings in water care should be taken to avoid bubbles which tend to attach themselves to the submerged wire and stone and thus falsify the results.

With the gravity bottle, or picrometer, the same result is arrived at in a slightly different way. The bottle is fitted with a ground glass stopper, pierced and sometimes furnished with a tube of small caliber, through which water which previously nearly or quite filled the bottle is forced when the stopper is inserted. The whole design of the gravity bottle is to provide a receptacle that can be accurately filled with water, the surplus moisture being carefully removed from the outside with blotting paper, paper towel or a linen cloth.

The weight of the stone is first determined. Let us call this A. Next the weight of the bottle exactly full of water is taken and set aside as B. The stone is then placed in the bottle, from which it displaces an amount of water exactly equal to its size, and the weight of the bottle accurately filled with the stone and water is determined. Denote this by C. Now it is perfectly evident that the combined weight of the bottle full of water and the stone weighed separately less the weight of the bottle full of water with the stone inside represents the weight of an amount of water exactly equal to the stone in volume. So we have as an expression for the specific gravity of the stone (G):—

$$G = \frac{A}{A+B-C}$$

Care should be taken to avoid the possibility of bubbles of air forming in the bottle, and to avoid also any slight change of temperature of the water due to handling the bottle. As a precaution against the latter source of error a handkerchief should be used to prevent the hands from touching the bottle directly.

Where the determination of relative weight for a number of

stones is required to be made quickly and frequently, a series of standardized liquids, such as mixtures of methylene iodide and benzol, may be prepared to cover a range of relative weights embracing many of the gem stones. They will be found of value, particularly as a means of differentiating certain stones. A description of these heavy liquids and of the method of using them will be found in most of the text books on mineralogy and gem stones.

The properties of gem minerals which depend on the way in which light is transmitted through the thickness of stones cut from them are to be reckoned among the useful tests for transparent gems. Those of us who are at all familiar with that most fascinating of sciences, the study of minerals, will recall how our interest in the mineral calcite was enhanced by noticing how pieces of the clear transparent Iceland spar showed us *two* images of everything viewed through them. This remarkable optical property, which we call *double refraction*, is to be seen at best in the Iceland spar variety of the mineral calcite, but other minerals, and among them several which are cut as gems, possess it to such a degree that double images of edges between the facets, or angular sides, at the bottom of a cut stone can be seen through the broad facet at the top by the aid of a hand lens, or even in some cases with the naked eye.

In this way we are able to tell easily and definitely the difference between a white diamond, which has no double refraction, and a white zircon, which has considerable.

A small white card may be used very effectively to show whether a cut stone throws back the mirror-like reflections of these bottom facets through the mass of the stone as single or double images. The stone is held in a patch of clear sunlight and its bright polished facets or sides are made to reflect the sun's image on the surface of the card, which is held about six inches away, and between the stone and the sun, just as the mirror of a heliostat is made to throw a reflection to a distant point. The facets that are nearest to the card (and to the sun) will, of course, reflect the sun's image without refraction, because the light does not pass *through* the stone, but the sun's rays which are reflected from the more distant facets (the back facets in the case where the top of the stone is presented to the sun) must pass through the thickness of the stone; and should the latter consist of a doubly refracting mineral, *two* reflections from these facets will be thrown on the card. By turning the stone slightly in different directions, the position in which the maximum effect is shown on the card is easily to be found. Where deep colored stones are to be tested in this way, it is best to use two cards, one with a hole cut in the center, behind which the stone is fastened with a little adhesive wax. The sunlight is allowed to pass directly through the stone, which registers its single or double refraction on the second card. By these devices not only are we enabled to detect quite small amounts of double refraction, but we can also roughly compare differences in the amount of this light property in different gem stones by noting the relative space between the two images on the card.

The card test serves to show us another property of light transmitted through gem stones that is useful in helping to identify them. Certain gem minerals possess more than others the property of splitting up the light rays that pass through them into the colors of the rainbow. It is this characteristic that gives to the cut diamond the flashes of color known as *fire*, which is one of its unique attractions. Dispersion, as this effect is called, is registered on the test card in the form of little rainbows of greater or less brilliancy and greater or less width, depending on the amount of dispersion characteristic of the particular gem stone tested.

CHAPTER II

"*Set me* . . . .
As a seal upon thine arm
For love is strong as death,
Jealousy is cruel as the grave."
—THE SONG OF SONGS VIII: 6

CHAPTER II

The Antique Use of Gems

A MONG the antique expressions of human culture which have been handed down to us through the ages, we find ample evidence that our prehistoric forebears began to appreciate the decorative value of gems and precious stones at an extremely early stage in their development.

The subtle charm that holds a twentieth century woman spellbound before a jeweler's window doubtless prompted Mother Eve to devise ways for hanging these vivid scraps of color about her person. So it happened that among the miscellaneous hodgepodge of articles of the bronze age excavated from a lake dweller grave in Bohemia were found a number of rough, uncut garnet pebbles, each pierced so that they could be strung together. Thus we have transmitted to us from before the very dawn of history this string of beads, like its present day survival in all but the polish and the facetting which our modern culture has given to the Bohemian garnets of this generation, and linking, as it were, the woman of today with her sister of the bronze age.

But the use of various minerals as materials from which objects for personal adornment were made, ancient though this use is, does not constitute the only side of the question of the antique use of gems. It is safe to assume that from the very earliest period when people began to recognize the beauty of certain stones they also ascribed to them certain supernatural properties as charms and talismans. And as far back as we can trace, they wore some material token in the form of a stone as an amulet to guard them from the ills of life, real or imaginary. The wearing of such amulets is, in all probability, older than the wearing of jewelry, and, no doubt, the one grew by insensible steps out of the other. It was essentially a natural and logical act for the primitive man who found an attractive or unusual bit of stone to ascribe to it occult powers. As he advanced in culture, he shaped these bits of stone into increasingly regular forms, and finally, as an added fetish, he scratched on them images of his gods and invocations to them.

Some of the earliest of these amulets are the little cylinders that were used as seals among the Assyrians, Babylonians, Persians and Hittites.

These cylinders, which date from about 5000 to about 400 B.C., are fashioned from various minerals such as steatite, serpentine, hematite, lapis lazuli, jasper, amazon stone, chalcedony, marble and rock crystal. Many of these materials are esteemed today for their beauty as mediums for small carvings, proving that modern taste in this matter is founded on ancient precedent.

The engraving was, of course, incised, both because this was the easiest and most obvious way of engraving hard materials, and because the impression made with such a seal was more natural and more easily distinguished. Considerable skill was displayed by these early lapidaries in cutting their designs, which consisted of figures of gods, man and animals, and also of inscriptions in cuneiform characters. The inscription often gave the name of the wearer, the name of his father and the name of his god. The seals of this type were not set in rings as are our present day seals, but were hung around the neck, or fastened on the arm, and consequently we find all of them pierced through the axis of the cylinder as though they were cylindrical beads.

A typical example is a Babylonian cylinder carved from limpid rock crystal, and roughly 3000 years old. This is engraved with a figure of a storm god Rammon, who was identical with the Rimmon of the Old Testament (2 Kings V: 18). He is here represented in a short robe, holding a scepter in one hand, and with the other drawn back. On each side of the god is represented his wife, Sahla, in a long flounced dress, and with both hands raised.

In Egypt the amulet took the form of the well known scarabæus or "scarab," a variation that strongly reflected the love for symbolization which characterized Egyptian culture. These little carved beetles were engraved as were the Asiatic seals, the inscription being cut on the oval under side of the conventualized figure in pictorial characters characteristic of Egyptian writing.

Scarabs were more typically amulets than were the cylinder seals of Babylon and Assyria, for they were commonly inscribed with magical charms taken from the Book of the Dead, and figured prominently in the burial customs of ancient Egypt. Carnelian, a quartz variety largely represented as a gem stone among many primitive peoples, seems to have been highly prized as a material for amulets in the earlier stages of Egyptian culture.

The beautifully worked funeral scarabs were often made from green jasper, amethyst, lapis lazuli, amazon stone, carnelian and serpentine, while the more precious emerald, ruby and turquoise are not without representation among these figures of the sacred beetle that replaced the heart in the mummies of the Egyptian dead. A powerful charm took the form of an eye usually fashioned from lapis lazuli, carnelian, chalcedony or amazon stone.

A form of engraved amulet that was much used in Persia is of the broad flat type, known as a Persian seal. These are made from flat slabs of chalcedony and carnelian, varying in size and shape, but rarely over 2½ inches in longest dimension. They are mostly oval or more rarely cushion shaped. The larger and more elaborate have a broad heart-shaped outline, and are sometimes mounted in silver with a ring by which they can be suspended from the neck.

The Mohammedan code forbids the depicting of natural objects such as men or beasts, so the engravers of these amulets were restrained from using the symbolism found among those of other cultures. All of them are engraved, as a consequence, in Arabic characters with texts from the Koran, the engraving in many instances being beautifully executed. The quaint Arabic letters, that look for all the world like some glorified kind of short hand, are highly decorative, and were embellished with loving care by the Muslem engraver. We are here somewhat reminded of the thoughtful pains with which the monkish scribes of the middle ages lettered their parchments.

The smaller examples are wrought with incised characters, often deeply cut as though for use as seals. But the larger and more beautiful kinds are cut with the lettering very slightly raised against a matte background composed of fine crossed lines, so that the inscription stands out in a polished surface against a dead one. Nothing can be more beautiful than the exquisite delicacy and detail of this engraving as revealed when the light strikes across the polished face of the lettering. The effect is much the same, and achieved in the same way, as that which one sees on an old engraved sword blade.

It is quite frequent among the engraved chalcedony amulets of this flat seal type to find a short text, or sometimes only the name of the Prophet, occupying the center of the design, and a longer text wrought as a border or panel around it. Also we meet with considerable repetition, a text of notable efficacy as a charm being used on many amulets.

The more richly engraved among the Persian seal amulets date from the sixteenth or seventeenth centuries, and represent an advanced phase of Muslem culture. Many of the smaller examples, however, are much older, dating from the eighth or tenth centuries.

It is impossible to contemplate these old fragments of a vivid and picturesque civilization without mentally stepping back into the days of the Arabian Nights. As with all relics of the past, they call to us with no uncertain voice and fire our imagination no less than they claim our appreciation as works of art. Particularly is this true of a little square seal of red burnt tile now in a famous collection. This is inscribed with Kufic characters, like those in which the early manuscripts of the Koran are said to have been written, and might have been worn upon the person of more than one among the fanatical followers of the Prophet.

Of the present day forms of jewelry the necklace is without question the most ancient. From such rough assemblages of strung-together gem pebbles as the garnets of the Bohemian lake dweller, mentioned several pages back, to the most elaborate creations of the modern jeweler, we can trace in unbroken sequence through the ages and in most of the countries of the ancient world the evolution of the necklace. The units that compose some of the most barbaric of these old strings of beads are only roughly worked, as for example the Persian necklace pictured at the end of the chapter. With higher development in culture such as is found among the Egyptian jewelry of about 2000 B.C., the gem stone beads were better rounded and polished. Here too we find a considerable scope in the materials used, amethyst, lapis lazuli, carnelian, turquoise, jasper, rock crystal, garnet and even emerald being freely combined with gold to produce jewelry forms of great taste and charm. It is quite significant that where regular crystal forms characterize the material, such as the hexagonal prisms of emerald, these forms seem to be preserved intact in the bead design, and whereas the beads fashioned from amethyst, carnelian or amazon stone were spherical or cylindrical, the six-sided prisms of emerald were simply pierced in the direction of their axes and left otherwise unworked.

The reason for this may lie in the reluctance of the artificer to waste any of the material of the rarer and consequently more precious stone, or possibly some symbolism was attached to its regular natural shape.

The Gallo-Roman strings of beads of the Merovingian epoch present fine examples of the use of agate for the fashioning of beads of this culture. These somewhat barbaric necklaces, the heavier of which were probably worn by men, possess a certain unique beauty and delicacy of color which strongly appeals to our modern taste.

From the necklace composed of strung beads it is but a step to one in which the roughly shaped stones were encased in a metal setting. In Egyptian neck jewelry we find this advance taking place at quite an early stage, as instanced by an example in the collection of the Metropolitan Museum of Art, where a small square plaque of gold enclosing an oval carnelian forms the central element of a double string of unset carnelian beads. At a somewhat later period we find the Egyptians using a sort of mosaic of gem stones, turquoise and lapis lazuli, set in thin gold boxes, shaped to the design, so that the whole has somewhat the aspect of the cloisonne work of Russia.

The transition from such primitive combinations of gem stones with the precious metals to the more elaborate settings of **Greece** and **Rome** is both easy and obvious, and once made, the development of jewelry forms is simply a matter of historic and political progress. As the needs of an ever advancing civilization called for more and more varied ornamentation of the dress and person in gold and silver, it was inevitable that these ornaments should be embellished with the gem stones that had already become familiar to man through the medium of earlier and simpler jewelry forms.

A striking instance of this adaptation of the earlier to the later usage is to be found in the necklace that constitutes the ceremonial trapping of a Vizier of Morocco of the middle of the eighteenth century. The roughly rounded aquamarines that furnish the larger jewels for this regalia are pierced, clearly indicating that they were once strung together to form a necklace of a much earlier and more primitive type; how much earlier we have no means of knowing.

And so we come to a very interesting consideration concerning the antiquity of gem stones, that is, what has become of the jewelry of our ancestors? Some of it, of course, has passed on to descendants and survives as family heirlooms, but comparatively little of it is accounted for in this way. A goodly proportion of it finds its way into the hands of the buyer of old jewelry, and the good stones are resold, reset and perhaps recut. A lapidary would tell us that a fair proportion of his raw material is made up of these "old stones," which he recuts.

In fact, nothing is quite so indestructible as a gem stone. It persists in being an emerald, or a sapphire, or an amethyst, and nothing else.

Much of the supply of fine peridots which come to the gem market every year are brought from the Island of St. John in the Red Sea, where they are washed up on the beach with other pebbles. But, and this is significant, many of them before they are recut for modern use show conclusively that they once played a similar part in ancient Greek jewelry.

It would be interesting if we could trace the history of every gem in a jeweler's show case. Some of them may have been mined only last year, but others may be centuries old. Rarely if ever is a gem that has once been cut, destroyed. It never wears out. If not buried with its owner, it must pass on to decorate the person of some one of the next generation. And even when buried, it may be dug up to continue its career, inciting to love and hate, greed and murder. Gold and silver objects are ultimately melted up and shaped into something else. A gem never loses its distinct character as such. The emeralds that graced Cleopatra are probably in existence somewhere in the world today.

AN EARLY PERSIAN NECKLACE
This string of necklace beads was fashioned from rough lumps of lapis lazuli,
brought by the trading caravans from Afghanistan.

Courtesy of American Museum of Natural History

A PERSIAN AMULET
Carved from chalcedony and engraved
with texts from the Koran. The Arabic
lettering has the effect of an intricate
and beautiful decoration.

Courtesy of American Museum of Natural History

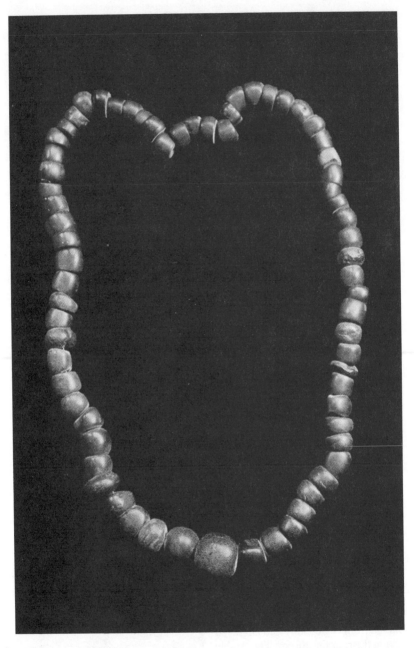

A necklace of ancient amber beads, from a grave of the Fourth Century, B.C., in Hallstatt, Austria. Baltic amber beads, such as this string, were a standard medium of exchange among the Germanic tribes of that period.

Courtesy of American Museum of Natural History

Like a skilled surgeon, the diamond lapidary performs the delicate operation which is known as "slitting." Just the right amount of the stone, no more and no less, must be split away. The intent expression on the face of the operator bears witness to the momentous effect of the slight blow he is about to strike on the steel knife edge which he holds in his left hand.

Author Photo

Even the refuse from this operation is valuable and must be saved. As the lapidary rough-shapes his diamonds, rubbing or "bruting" the one on the end of the long stick which he holds under his right arm, against the other on the rapidly turning spindle which is driven by the belt, the dust and fine fragments fall into the little box shown in the centre of the picture.

Author Photo

The tools of the diamond lapidary's art are very simple. The little metal cut or "dop," in which the diamond is being placed, as well as the wooden holder which carries it, are of exactly the same shape as those used by the diamond cutters of a hundred years ago.

Author Photo

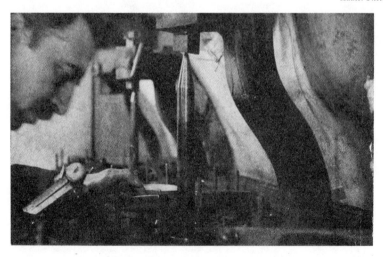

The actual cutting of the facets on the diamond, known as "polishing," calls for the highest expression of the diamond lapidary's art. The stems of the "dops," which bear the diamonds, must be adjusted in the "tongs" with fine nicety. Here again the form of the tools has not changed in a century. The appliances shown are the same as those used in Antwerp in 1836.

Author Photo

CHAPTER III

"There are at this mine numerous diamond cutters, and each has only a steel wheel of about the size of our plates. They place but one stone on each wheel, and pour water incessantly on the wheel until they have found the grain of the stone. The grain being found, they pour on oil and do not spare diamond dust, although it is costly, in order to make the stone run faster, and they weight it more heavily than we do."

—VOYAGES DE TAVERNIER (1676)

CHAPTER III

The Art of the Lapidary

LTHOUGH a gem mineral in the rough always exhibits certain qualities which, to a discerning eye, give promise of its possibilities as a gem, it is through the shaping and facetting of these bits of mineral that their real charm is developed. Gem stones are, in general, cut

1—To bring out beauties of color.

2—To adapt them to jewelry forms.

3—To develop the scintillating reflections from the interior of the stone by making use of the principles of refraction of light.

The first two of these considerations are too obvious to require more than a word of explanation. The surface of a transparent uncut gem stone may be compared to the surface of a body of water rendered rough and broken by waves and ripples. It is only when such a surface has been rendered smooth that we are enabled to look down into the depths below and see to best advantage its color. The stones which embellish a piece of jewelry must have a regularity of outline and a symmetry in the disposal of their planes and angles in order best to please the eye.

The third reason for the cutting of planes or facets on transparent gem stones needs rather more explanation. We have no doubt many times had occasion to admire the brilliant flashes of light reflected back from the interior of a diamond without realizing how this effect was produced; indeed, the reason why a diamond glistens is to most of us a deep mystery. When we put a spoon in a glass of water and hold it above the level of the eye we can see a reflection of the submerged part of the spoon from the under side of the surface of the water which acts as a mirror. Now the light that falls on the upper surface of a correctly cut diamond is reflected back to the eye from the smooth *under* surfaces of the stone in just the same way that the spoon is reflected from the surface of the water in the glass. In Figure 1 the paths traversed by some of these rays of light are shown, and it will be seen that they are reflected from the angular sides of the diamond in much the same way that a billiard ball is deflected from the cushions of a billiard table. It is important that the facets should have the correct inclination to one another in order that no light should "leak out" from the under side of the stone, and it is here that the lapidary, that is the person who cuts the stone, must take into account its *index of refraction.* By this we mean the amount of bending that light undergoes when it enters obliquely one substance, such as water or diamond, from another, such as air. Because the refraction of diamond is so high, light, having passed

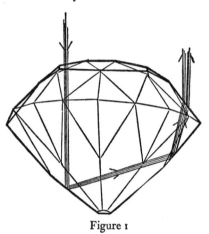

Figure 1

through it, must "hit" a surface from the inside much more squarely than would be the case with another substance, such as glass, in order to pass back into air. To insure that all the light that falls on the upper surface of a cut diamond shall be reflected, we have only to proportion the stone so that the facets of the under side will have the proper inclination, and our diamond will glisten like a star. But a diamond does something more to light than merely reflect it. It also tends to split up the white light into the colors of the spectrum, so that mixed with the brilliant flashes of white light we also have gleams of all the colors of the rain-

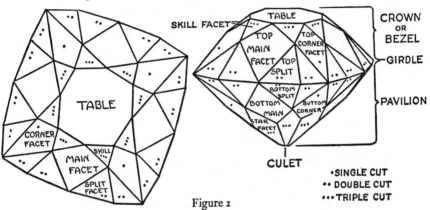

Figure 2

bow sent back to the eye from our cut stone, which is very properly called a brilliant.

The upper part of a brilliant is called the *crown* or *bezel*, and the lower part is known as the *pavilion;* the line separating the crown from the pavilion and marking the widest part of the stone is the *girdle*. The size of the girdle constitutes the *spread* of the stone, and the crown and pavilion taken together constitute its *depth*. There are also special names given to the various kinds of facets. These are given in diagram in Figure 2.

When we come to consider the methods and tools of gem cutting, we encounter a sharply defined boundary between these methods and tools as applied to the cutting of diamonds and those used in the fashioning of other and softer gems. This difference of treatment is imposed in the case of diamond by the special difficulty to be met in grinding and polishing facets on such an exceedingly hard substance.

We will then begin our little excursion into the side of gem knowledge that deals with the way gem stones are treated at the hands of the lapidary by following a diamond on its journey from the mine to the jeweler and seeing for ourselves just what happens to it. When the diamonds are taken out of the mine, not by any means all of them are clear and colorless, as self respecting diamonds should be; indeed, only about 25 percent of the stones found are without some faint color. Of the remainder about one third are of a light shade of violet, yellow or brown, and are known as "off color" stones. The remainder, roughly one half of the total find, are more or less deeply colored and are consequently of no value for jewelry, although still usable as diamond dust for cutting and polishing and also for the cutting edges or facings for rock drills. So we find that at the beginning of its travels the diamond is introduced to the sorter. The sorter is a kind of a super-expert on diamonds whose eye has been trained through years of practice to detect the slightest variations in the color of diamonds, and to find flaws in stones with an ease which is little less than uncanny. Safeguarded behind a heavy metal screen, the diamond appraiser sits with a pile of rough stones before him, judging each stone and assigning it to its proper heap.

The first consideration in sorting diamonds is the adaptability of the stone for cutting. Let us assume that the stone whose travels we are following is sorted into the grade known as "close goods," comprising complete, flawless crystals from which fair-sized brilliants can be cut, to use the trade term, "made." These usually have eight sides or faces, triangular in shape. Next comes a resorting of the "close goods" into eight grades, ranging from blue-white, which comprises the stones of finest quality, to yellow and brown crystals, which are so badly off-color as to be unfit for gems. If our stone has passed the critical test of the sorter and has been placed in one of the higher grades, it is weighed, wrapped up in a parcel with others of its kind, a price per carat is assigned to it, and it is sold to a diamond dealer, and ultimately finds its way to the workshop of the diamond polisher. Here, at the hands of a highly skilled workman, it is destined to be turned into a gem fit to grace beauty or proclaim opulence.

Much of this work is done in Holland and especially in Amsterdam, which since the fifteenth century has been famous for this industry, which is in reality an art. But there are, nevertheless, a number of shops in operation in New York and in other American cities. Like many other operators who depend for their success on a high degree of manual skill, the diamond cutter uses few tools, and these are relatively primitive and have changed but little since the days of Louis de Bequem, who cut diamonds as early as 1475. The lapidary trained in his art depends, like the violin player, on the delicacy of his touch, and, like the painter, on the accuracy of his eye. In general he does not employ complex mechanical devices to aid him in his difficult task.

The surface irregularities, which are often present on diamonds of even the highest quality, must be first split away from the stone, which breaks naturally along smooth, even surfaces parallel to the natural faces of an octahedron. Superficial flaws, that is, incipient cracks and dark patches or "carbons," must also be eliminated in this way. Sometimes these occur deep in the center of an otherwise perfect crystal, in which case the diamond is divided *through* the imperfection and made into two or more cut stones. To accomplish this cleavage, which is known as "slitting," our diamond is firmly cemented to the end of a wooden stick, which, in turn, is supported firmly in an upright position by wedging it into a hole in the working bench. The diamond lapidary now makes a deep scratch in just the right place upon the surface of the diamond crystal, using for this purpose the sharp corner of a diamond fragment. A knife edge is then held in the correct position on the scratch, and a sharp blow with a light tool struck on the back of the knife edge suffices to remove the undesirable flake, leaving the surface bright and very smooth.

Sometimes, when the stone is large, it is of advantage to saw it into two or more pieces so as to save as much as possible of the weight in cut diamonds. This is accomplished with a thin disk of bronze, about four inches in diameter, revolving very rapidly and having its edge charged with diamond dust at the beginning of the sawing. As the saw bites into the stone, it keeps recharging itself with the diamond sawdust. It takes many hours for this little "buzz saw" to eat its way through half an inch of diamond, but the finished product is so valuable that a day or so of labor makes little impression on the cost sheet.

The rough shaping of the diamond is done through an operation called "bruting," which consists of wearing away the corners by rubbing one stone against another. Formerly this was strictly a manual process, the two diamonds being mounted on sticks held in either hand by the lapidary. Even into the ancient and conservative art of diamond cutting, however, some mechanical improvements have made their way, and now in most of the shops a rapidly twirling spindle takes the place of one of the hand sticks. The remaining stick has grown in length to suit the modern method. It is now about two feet long and can be firmly grasped with both hands and held in a rest so that the diamond it bears at its end can be rubbed against its fellow, which is spinning in front of it.

Having in this manner rough-shaped our diamond, we now come to the finishing operation, the producing of the facets which give brilliancy and sparkle to it, an operation which is technically known as polishing. The holder of the stone during the polishing consists of a small metal cup on a long stem, which is called a "dop" and much resembles a tulip, which famous Dutch flower may have suggested its shape. A solder composed of one part tin and three parts lead is placed in the dop and heated until soft. The diamond is then embedded in the solder with the portion of the stone on which the desired facets are to be cut placed uppermost. When the diamond has been properly adjusted in the dop, it is plunged in cold water to cool and harden the solder. Such drastic treatment would cause less aristocratic stones promptly to fly to pieces, but not so with the diamond; the high heat conductivity of this remarkable mineral permits it to submit to the sudden change of temperature without there resulting in it even the slightest flaw.

The dop is now fastened by means of its stem in a heavy iron arm, called the tongs, in such a way as to bring the position of the facet to be cut exactly undermost when it is placed in contact with the polishing wheel or "skeep." It is here that the skill and training of the diamond cutter is exercised to its fullest, for the tilt or inclination of the various facets, the one to the other, depends on the position of the dop in the tongs and on just how much the stem of the former is bent to the one side or to the other.

The skeep is made of soft iron and turns horizontally at the rate of about 2500 revolutions a minute. Diamond dust mixed with olive oil is fed to this wheel, and the diamond is held in contact with it by the weight of the tongs aided by slabs of lead placed upon the latter. Much care has to be taken to keep the skeep perfectly balanced so that it will revolve without the slightest rocking motion, because this would materially interfere with the even smoothness of run necessary to the production of a finely polished surface. Several hours are required to cut one facet. Then the dop is readjusted for another one, or the stone is removed and reset in the dop, and so on until all of the fifty-eight little faces, in which lie the secret of the brilliancy of the jewel, are produced.

To appreciate the exquisite skill and infinite patience involved in this apparently simple process, we have only to look at the gem on our finger sending forth its magical fires, and to note the symmetry and regularity of shape of each of its tiny glittering sides. And when we remember that to produce these rainbow-like rays each facet must have exactly the right tilt with respect to its neighbors, we realize that a cut diamond is not only a wonderful product of nature but a marvelous work of art.

The cutting of the softer gem stones is not nearly so laborious an undertaking as the cutting of diamonds. Not only is diamond harder than any other substance known, but it is very much harder than the corundum gem stones that follow next after it in hardness. So it is that we find the tools and methods applied to the softer gem stones at once simpler and more highly manual.

The native lapidaries of India and Ceylon have reduced the apparatus of this phase of gem cutting to its lowest terms. Such a native artisan, seated on his carpet in the bazaar, turns the stone lap in front of him by the primitive means of a bow, the string of which is wrapped around the axle of his stone grinding wheel. By his side is a bowl containing the emery he uses as a grinding medium mixed to the right consistency with water, and his left hand is the only holder for the gem stone that he is manipulating. This is indeed reducing the tools of gem cutting to an absolute minimum, and emphasizing in a striking way the essentials of this art.

These essentials are then:—

1—A rapidly revolving wheel, the flat surface of which is of just the proper roughness for retaining the powdered abrasive with which the cutting of the smooth facets of a gem stone is accomplished. This wheel is usually termed a lap.

2—A holder, corresponding to the dop used in diamond polishing, but in this instance made of wood and resembling in size and shape an old-fashioned pen holder.

3—An abrasive substance of a greater degree of hardness than the gem stone to be cut, which is fed to the lap as a powder mixed with water to a more or less thin paste. For the final polishing the abrasive is fed dry to a wooden or cloth covered lap.

Gem stones are first sawed or "slit" by means of a thin disk of relatively soft metal whose edge is slightly indented with a knife blade for its entire circumference. Diamond dust mixed to a paste with water, is fed to this circular saw, and, lodging in the indentations of the circumference, constitutes the cutting edge. The process of slitting for colored stones is very much more rapidly accomplished than the corresponding operation for diamonds, and, except in the case of valuable gem stones such as rubies and sapphires, no great amount of care is taken to conserve the chips taken off.

After a suitable piece, free from flaws and other blemishes, and of convenient proportions, has been sawed from the crystal

or rough fragment of gem material, this piece is usually cemented
to the end of a wooden holder for the rough shaping, which cor-
responds to the "blocking out" of a painting. This is done against
an emery or carborundum wheel, resembling a small grindstone
and revolving on a horizontal axis. If the stone is to be given a
cabochon or rounded cutting like an opal or a cat's eye, it is
finished on this wheel and polished on a similar one of softer
material charged with rouge or putty powder. If, however, the
stone is to be facetted, the real skill and judgment of the lapidary
is called into play. The rough shaped stone is attached with cement to the blunt end of a wooden holder, called the stick, which
is about 8 or 10 inches long and which is pointed at its free end.
The position of the stone when fastened to the stick is so chosen
that the table facet when cut will be at right angles to the stick,
and the stone is embedded in the cement up to the point where
the prospective girdle will encircle it.

The grinding lap, which is made of gun metal, copper or lead,
depending on the hardness of the stone to be facetted, is mounted
so as to revolve in a horizontal plane, like the skeep used in polishing diamonds, and the speed at which its surface travels *against*
the stone can be manipulated with greater nicety by moving the
latter nearer to or farther from the center. Having charged his
lap with the appropriate abrasive, emery or carborundum, the
lapidary now places the stone upon the surface of the wheel and,
holding the stick in a vertical position, grinds the table facet to
its correct proportion with respect to the design of facets which
he has in mind.

The next step is to cut the first of the main facets of the crown,
which of course necessitates the holding of the stick at just the
right angle to the surface of the wheel, and as a rough guide the
lapidary is here aided by a device called the "jamb peg" mounted

at the side of the lap and pivoted so as to swing out over it. The jamb peg is shaped somewhat like an elongated peg top and is furnished with a series of shallow indentations at regular intervals from top to bottom, so that by placing the sharpened end of the stick in one of these a constant angle between the stick and the surface of the lap can be maintained. Having cut the first of the main facets of the crown to the right depth, the lapidary now turns the stick through just the right arc of a circle to bring the next facet to bear on the surface of the lap, and using the same hole in the jamb peg, cuts this also to the correct depth, constantly inspecting his work and judging the fine points of inclination and proportion of the facets by eye. But since he can not see what is taking place while the stone is in contact with the lap, he must here depend on a highly developed sense of touch. Just as the finger of a violinist flies unerringly to the precise spot on the neck of his instrument to produce a given note, so the trained touch of the lapidary guiding the stick that holds his gem upon the wheel finds almost by instinct the correct angle for the stone to come in contact with the grinding surface to produce the result he desires.

One after the other the main, split and skill facets are cut, and then the stone goes to the polisher, who, working in the same way but on a lap having a softer and finer surface, and using a finer abrasive, removes the slight scratches from the facets, polishes them to a finished brilliancy and incidentally corrects any slight irregularity in their proportion. Because of this last consideration it follows that the polisher must be a master in his craft.

The crown or upper half of the stone having thus been completed, it is now removed from the stick, cleaned and again mounted in cement, but this time with the lower half exposed on the end of the stick. The process of cutting and polishing is now repeated for the pavilion facets, and the stone is finished.

A word as to the modern methods of carving jade and other hard decorative stones, as these arts are practised in China.

In all the manual arts the artist depends upon perfection of skill in the execution of his work rather than upon elaborate tools or accessories. The same kind of brushes, the same form of palette, and, to a large extent, the same pigments with which Raphael wrought his masterpieces would serve equally well the painter of today.

A modern violin virtuoso actually prefers to play upon an instrument made by Stradivarius two hundred and fifty years ago. It is because the tools of these arts are simple that we have not improved upon them; because the hand and the eye are so essential that they are hampered rather than aided by mechanical contrivances. It is said that Ruskin produced his best etching with the broken tine of a steel fork.

What is true of all the manual arts is especially and significantly true as applied to the carving of small objects executed by the Chinese and the Japanese.

Between these two groups of artisans there are certain essential differences. The Japanese express their glyphic sense mainly through the medium of ivory and wood. The sole exception to this generalization, if we may call it an exception, is the fashioning of polished spheres from rock crystal.

On the other hand, Chinese carvers work chiefly in the decorative stones such as jade, rock crystal, amethyst, chalcedony, jasper, rose quartz, carnelian, turquoise, lapis lazuli, not to mention softer mediums such as serpentine, malachite and amber.

Again, whereas the Japanese artists employ an elaborate realism, albeit often with a certain grotesque humor, the lapidaries of China conventionalize their subjects, frequently developing this conventionalization into a symbolism rich in significance and beauty.

The ivory and wood carvers of Japan sign their work, thus handing down their names to posterity; whereas the masterpiece of a Chinese lapidary, however elaborately or skillfully it may be wrought, is never signed. It would almost seem as though to the patient and highly skilled artists of the Flowery Kingdom the execution of an admirable work constitutes its own reward.

The most ancient as well as the most interesting medium employed by Chinese lapidary artists is the group of mineral varieties known as jade. At present the sources of raw material for Chinese carved jade are as various as the material itself. From the Khotan district of Eastern Turkestan comes the white or nearly white nephrite known as *ti*. The dark green colors include nephrite from the neighborhood of Lake Baikal, and the opaque brighter green jadeite from Yunnan. The choicest emerald green jadeite known to us as *imperial jade* is mined in the Mogaung district in upper Burmah.

Simple as are the tools of the modern Chinese carver of jade, they are probably many steps in advance of those used prior to K'ien Lung Dynasty. With the reign of the Emperor K'ien Lung in 1736, Chinese art experienced a renaissance which in the instance of jade carving found expression in a supple and intricate technique.

In all probability the advent of this impulse toward more elaborate work in jade carving found the lapidaries using some primitive form of rotary drill, probably aided and supplemented by incised tool work, such as we find the world over in early carved work in hard stones.

Today the block of jade is cut into slices by an iron wire drawn across from side to side, a liberal supply of abrasive mixed with water being supplied to the cutting wire. A circular disk of metal, rotated in alternating directions by foot treadles and also served with abrasive, is used to rough shape the piece much as a draughtsman would use charcoal roughly to outline a design.

The design in relief and what undercutting is necessary are executed with wheels of various sizes and thicknesses, all operated by the simple device of a broad belt passing over the spindle of the cutting wheel and drawn backward and forward by the pressure of the feet on treadles.

When the design has been cut, the same device serves to rotate the polishing tools, disks made of fine grained wood or gourd skin, or oxleather rolled into narrow but thick rolls and smeared with ruby dust.

The intricate patterns of openwork which characterize many of the pendants and belt ornaments of the K'ien Lung period were achieved by numberless holes drilled through the thin jade plates in the corners of the design by the use of diamond drills operated by a wrapped bowstring. The holes thus made were connected by cuts made with wire saws, which neatly sawed out the piece represented by the opening.

The hollow which constitutes the inside of a snuff bottle is always cut before the outer surface. A hole is bored by means of a tubular drill, which is rotated with a bow string to the depth needed. Then small lap wheels inserted through the neck gradually work out the shape of the inside surface. Some of the contours of these inside surfaces are by no means simple, such elaborations as hour-glass contractions and square shoulders leaving us completely mystified as to how any rotating tool could have shaped them. The difficulty of the inside of the bottle having been successfully overcome, the outer surface presents no hardships, being treated with various wheels like any other object.

For abrasives, the Chinese lapidary uses (a) yellow sand (quartz); (b) red sand (garnet); (c) black sand (emery); (d) jewel dust (powdered ruby).

It is with the last of these that the semi-final polishing is accomplished, the actual final polish being acquired by years of fingering and rubbing in the hands of generations of Chinese who are the fortunate owners of such a piece.

These are the bare outlines of the jade carver's methods. It sounds simple, and so does the drawing of a bow across a violin string sound simple. One must remember that there are no sketches preceding these works of art. They must all be visualized before tool touches stone, and there must be no slip or mistake in the execution of the design. Patience, almost infinite patience, is the price paid for their perfection—such patience as none but an Oriental can attain, and no Westerner can even vaguely realize.

CHAPTER IV

"And they were stronger hands than mine
That digged the ruby from the earth,
More cunning brains that made it worth
The large desire of a king."
                              —RUDYARD KIPLING

CHAPTER IV

Forms in which Gems are Cut

THE HISTORY of gem cutting, insofar as it touches the modern art of the lapidary, may be said to begin with the introduction of diamonds as personal ornaments into Europe about the fifteenth century. It is perfectly true that precious stones were worn upon the person of men and women at a period which carries us well back into prehistoric times, and it is possible to trace a certain rough fashioning in even the most antique of these. But, aside from the question of whether the early gem artifacts were worn for purely esthetic reasons, or, as is more probable, for charms endowed with a certain occult potency, the fact remains that up to a comparatively late period no attempt was made in shaping a gem to do more than adapt its outline to the form of setting designed for it, and to round off its corners and irregularities so that its color might be seen to the best advantage.

In tracing the development of gem cutting in general, we are led inevitably for a point of departure to the forms first produced in the cutting of diamonds, because these early diamond cuttings impressed their character and symmetry not only upon later developed forms of cutting adapted to diamonds, but to the subsequent development of forms of cutting among all the other transparent gem stones.

We have the authority of O. M. Dalton, in the "Catalogue of Finger Rings in the British Museum," for the statement that previous to Louis de Bequem, that is, prior to the latter half of the fifteenth century, four of the eight faces of an octahedral diamond crystal were sometimes polished and the stone set with the polished pyramid projecting, while the unpolished portion of the stone was imbedded in the setting. The next step in advance of this very obvious and primitive facetting was to brut two diamond crystals together until the operator had worn away one of the points of the octahedron into a square facet, corresponding to a table in the modern brilliant, and similarly had worn a smaller facet on the opposite point corresponding to the culet. This earliest of diamond cutting is shown in Figure 3. Frequently the culet was omitted and the table was developed to even a smaller extent than shown. We have reason to believe that this modified point cut persisted at least into the seventeenth century, inasmuch as a ring dating from this period in the British Museum collection is set with a diamond cut in this way.

Aside from the fact that the modified point cutting utilized the maximum spread and a large proportion of the maximum weight of a given stone, the square girdle produced a certain awkwardness, which subsequently led to the modifying of this form by the cutting away of the corner edges both in the crown and the pavilion, and to the production of an octagonal girdle.

As a finished expression of the diamond cutter's art this form of cutting, which is shown in Figure 4, and which is sometimes called single cut, has long been obsolete; it is, however, interesting to note that in the evolution of a modern brilliant cut, the diamond crystal or cleaved piece passes through both of the preceding forms as its initial stages before the split, star and skill facets are

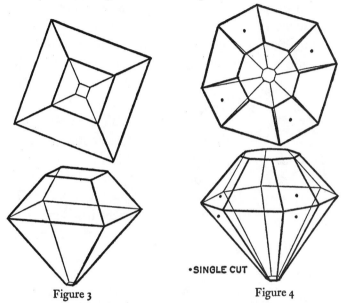

Figure 3   Figure 4

•SINGLE CUT

produced. It would seem fair then to consider both of these cuttings as old forms of brilliant cut.[1]

About the middle of the seventeenth century a development of the two previous forms of cutting into what has been variously called the square cut brilliants, single-cut brilliants,[2] or double cut brilliants,[3] took place. The first of these forms, Figure 5, which we will call the square cut brilliant, retains the original square table of Figure 3; the top main facet of a single cut starting from the corner of the table making with the single cut an octagonal girdle, the corners of which are taken off with the corner facets of a double cut starting from the same point. The

[1] See W. R. Catelle, The Diamond, Plate V, Figs. 1 and 2.
[2] Emanuel.
[3] Bauer.

main and corner facets are repeated in the pavilion, starting from a point on the edge corresponding to the corner of the table. This gives a brilliant of 34 facets, not without a certain amount of symmetry, particularly in the crown.

The English square-cut brilliant, or old English star-cut brilliant, Figure 6, is derived as in Figure 3, and with double cut

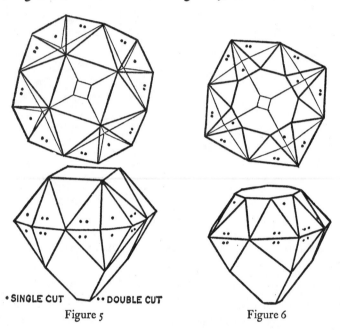

• SINGLE CUT ✳ •• DOUBLE CUT

Figure 5   Figure 6

corner facets developed as in the previous cutting. This gives a brilliant of 30 facets with an octagonal table and a rather more symmetrical grouping of the facets of the crown than any of the preceding cuttings. A somewhat later development of the double cut brilliant is shown in Figure 7. This is the connecting link between the single cut brilliant of Figure 4 and the various forms of the triple cut brilliant which will be presently discussed; the

edges between the main facets of the single cut being partly replaced in crown and pavilion each by two corner facets. This
gives a brilliant of 50 facets with much the same outline of the
girdle as has the Brazilian cut or Old Mine cut (Figure 9).

What the square-cut brilliants following the lines of the basic
octahedron failed to do was accomplished with the introduction

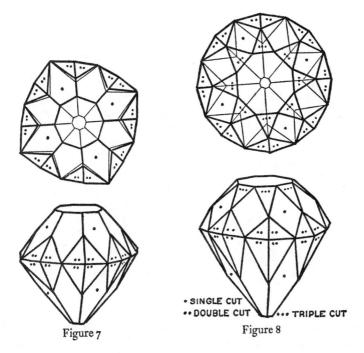

• SINGLE CUT
•• DOUBLE CUT   ••• TRIPLE CUT

Figure 7   Figure 8

of the triple cut brilliant toward the end of the seventeenth century and the beginning of cutting for brilliancy and weight rather
than for weight alone. Three variations of the triple cut brilliant
are of sufficient importance to be considered here.

The English round cut brilliant, of which an excellent description with relative proportions is to be found in Emanuel's "Dia-

monds and Precious Stones," was apparently in vogue in England
in the middle of the nineteenth century. This variation of the
triple cut brilliant (Figure 8) differs from the American brilliant
of today only in the relative proportions of its essential parts. In
it the angles of the octahedron were deviated from to produce
a stone of depth rather than spread, the "lumpy" aspect of the

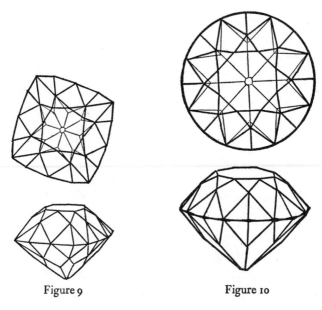

Figure 9   Figure 10

cutting being the result of making the diameter of the girdle
equal the total depth. The number of facets was increased to 58
by the addition of the skill facets in the crown, a change which
not only added to the symmetry of the exposed portion of the
cutting but increased the surface reflections. The essential inno-
vation, however, lay in the altering of the angles of the crown
and pavilion main facets to totally reflect a large proportion of
the light falling directly on the crown, these reflections mate-

rially adding to the brilliancy of the cutting. It is evident that the theory of this cutting necessitates rather a high crown with a relatively small table, and that some sacrifice is made of the spread of the stone so that for a given weight a stone of relatively small spread but considerable brilliancy is obtained.

The tendency to retain the girdle outline of the old square cut

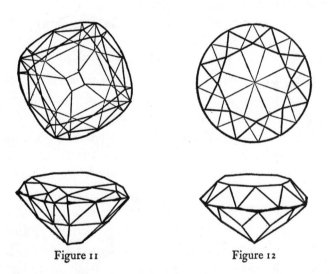

Figure 11   Figure 12

brilliants found expression in the Brazilian cut brilliant or Old Mine cut, which is shown in Figure 9, and which was very much in vogue during the last century at a period when Brazil was producing most of the world's diamonds. In the example shown, the angles between the main facets of the crown and pavilion approach more nearly in average to the ideal angle (80° to 85°) of the modern brilliant than in the English round cut brilliant, where this angle is over rather than under 90°. The result is a cutting of better because less "lumpy" proportions, and one in which thinner stones could be cut to better advantage.

The final stage in the evolution of an ideal brilliant cut takes the form of the American cut brilliant shown in Figure 10. This cutting combines the most satisfactory angles of the Old Mine cut in a brilliant with a round girdle, and although undoubtedly some of the weight of the uncut stone is sacrificed to brilliancy and prismatic reflections, a considerable spread, compared with the weight of the cut stone, is reached.

In tracing the evolution of the brilliant cut from its earliest and most primitive form down to the highly developed brilliant of our own day, we followed, as it were, the main line of evolution leading to the cutting most adaptable to stones of medium weight and general use. It must be clearly borne in mind, however, that in the course of this development forms of gem cuttings have sprung from the main line of advance at many points, some of these having achieved only a transient popularity in the past, and some representing variations which are still in use for stones adapted to certain settings. To anyone familiar with the great diversity of these variants from the well known brilliant form of cutting, the futility of attempting anything in the nature of a classification will be quite patent. In some instances, as in the case of the table cut, the variation is mainly one of proportion, while in other cases the forms of cutting are combinations of brilliant and step cut. For convenience in arranging the data collected, it has been thought best to divide roughly the variations of the brilliant into three groups, based partly on the adaptability of the cutting to jewelry forms. Grouped in this way we have:

(a) Cuttings with symmetrical or rounded girdles.
(b) The commoner forms of fancy cuttings.
(c) Unusual forms of fancy cuttings.

The first of these groups includes stones adapted to solitaire ring settings, for the centers of clusters, and in fact for every form of jewelry setting where a round, square, or six-sided stone is required.

Conspicuous among cuttings of this group is the square brilliant, a notable example of which is to be found in the Cullinan IV diamond, shown in Figure 11. Although of much the same girdle outline as the typical Brazilian cut, exemplified in the Regent diamond, this cutting differs widely in proportion from the older forms; the crown is shallow with a broad table, and a considerable mass of the stone lies below the girdle. The main facets of the pavilion were doubled, bringing the number of facets up to 66 and giving to the culet end of the stone the appearance of a step cut treatment.

The round double-cut brilliant snown in Figure 12, and known as the table cut, represents a degree of simplicity of cutting which strongly suggests the old English star-cut brilliant, from which it was possibly derived. The table cut has 33 facets and is characterized by a broad spread compared to the depth, and a shallow crown with a broad table. In the example studied for Figure 12, the proportion of spread to depth was 2 to 1, and the depth of the crown was about one-third the total depth. Thin diamonds were formerly made in this cut, which has little or no advantage other than a high proportion of spread to weight.

An extremely popular cutting for sapphires, rubies and the deeper colored semiprecious stones is the combination brilliant-step cut. An example, studied from a blue synthetic sapphire, is shown in Figure 13. This variation of the brilliant has a rather low crown, cut with the conventional 33 facets, and a deep pavilion of three tiers of stepped facets. The girdle-bottom main facets are shaped to the circular girdle by single triangular corner facets, as shown in the figure. For colored stones of high index of refrac-

tion the combination cutting is very effective, as it brings out
both the fire and the color of the gem, but like all forms involving
step cutting, it requires that the proportions and slope of the
pavilion facets should be carefully studied.

The six-sided cutting shown in Figure 14, although formerly
used to a limited extent for diamonds, has now almost entirely

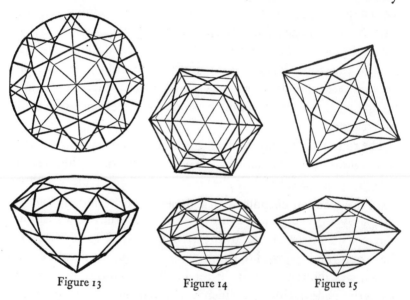

Figure 13   Figure 14   Figure 15

given way before the various forms of unmodified step cut. This
cutting is in reality a variation of step rather than in any sense a
form of brilliant cut; it is introduced here, however, because the
use of corner facets in the crown allies it to an extent with the
latter group. In the example shown in the figure the cutting produced rather a lumpy stone, in which about one-third of the total
depth lay above the girdle. Diamonds made in this cutting are
often met with in old-fashioned settings, and there is no doubt
that they possess a certain quaint charm; but unless very carefully

proportioned, much of the brilliancy of the stone is lost.

The French cut brilliant, illustrated in Figure 15, is principally used for small rubies, emeralds and sapphires when it is necessary to set these in a row for a bar pin or similar piece of jewelry. In this case of *calibre* cutting the square girdles of all of the stones constituting the setting must of course be made exactly the same size. For a small circlet, as in the instance of a diamond encircled by calibre-cut sapphires, the small stones are cut with a girdle which is slightly keystone-shaped to accommodate the curve of the circle. Like the preceding one, this cutting is closely allied in make to the step cut, being essentially a step cut with star facets in the crown.

In dealing with the great variety of fancy cuttings which are more or less derived from the brilliant cut, the difficulties in the way of arriving at anything approaching an adequate basis of classification are appreciably more than those met with in dealing with the group of cuttings with symmetrical or round girdles. At least in these latter we were guided by the outline of the stone and by the fact that most of the cuttings of this type were designed for setting in solitaire rings or for the centers or encircling elements or clusters. We now come to a group of cuttings of excentric girdle outlines, distorted from the round and with the brilliant cut crown, which alone ties them to the basis from which they are derived, pulled this way and that until the possible shapes producible as fancy cuttings seem endless. Another point of differentiation between this and the group previously discussed is that in the case of the fancy cuttings the stones are mostly adapted to settings other than rings, and that the cuttings are to a large extent used for the making of stones other than diamonds. A notable exception to both of these latter characterizations is that of the marquise cutting, which is used principally for diamonds and is almost universally set as a ring stone. The marquise was introduced as a cutting for diamonds early in the last decade of the nineteenth century, when popular taste in ring stones created a demand for a long narrow cutting intended to be set with the long axis parallel to the finger joints.

A typical example of a marquise cut diamond is to be found in

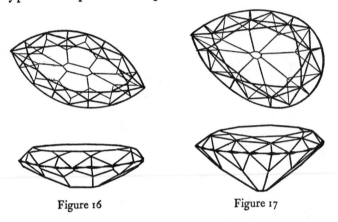

Figure 16   Figure 17

No. VII of the Cullinan cuttings, which weighs about 9½ carats. Figure 16 was studied from a model of this stone, and represents an average proportion between the length and breadth of girdle outline, which varies to a very considerable extent in this as in most of the other fancy cuttings. The 58 facets which constitute the *make* of the marquise correspond in relative position, facet for facet, with those of the round brilliant, the obvious distortion in shape of the facets being occasioned by the lengthening of one diameter of the type cutting. The broken arcs which outline the table are rendered more nearly circular by decreasing the size of the skill facets, so that instead of meeting corner to corner around the table, their edges with the table are alternated with edges of the top main facets.

The pendant cut, illustrated in Figure 17, is used for a great variety of precious and semiprecious stones. The example shown was studied from a model of the No. III Cullinan diamond, and may be taken as an average in proportion of length to breadth between the very broad pendant shapes, as exemplified in the Cullinan I diamond, and the very long slender pendants cut from small chrysoberyl. tourmalines or aquamarines. Whereas in the case of the marquise the variation from the round brilliant was produced by lengthening one diameter symmetrically, so in the pendant cut the variation consists in lengthening one end of a diameter of the type cutting. Pendant cut stones are very rarely, if ever, used for ring settings, and although a considerable proportion of the stones cut in this make are diamonds, it is very generally employed for all of the light-colored stones through a very wide range of weight.

Intimately related to the pendant-shaped brilliant is the heart-shaped brilliant, illustrated in Figure 18. This variation of the type brilliant cut might be considered as a pendant-shaped brilliant, with the round end somewhat flattened and with the girdle outline broadened until its length about equaled its breadth. In the present example, which was studied from a model of the No. V Cullinan diamond, the crown is shallow and the table relatively large.

No attempt has been made to work out the difficult problem of the optics of the three foregoing variations of the brilliant. There are so many elements to be considered where not even the girdle outline is a constant that we are led to suspect that the lapidaries and diamond cutters have no guiding rule, but make the stone to get the best advantage of weight and spread without considering the angles which give the maximum brilliancy. The three illustrations, chosen from the work of so distinguished a lapidary artist as Joseph Asscher, undoubtedly express a very close approximation to ideal proportions for their respective cuttings.

The extremely wide range of forms which are classed by lapidaries as fancy cutting precludes the discussion in a limited space of more than the essentially characteristic variations involving a treatment of the crown facets derived from the brilliant cut. With respect to the pavilion facets these fancy shapes have for the most

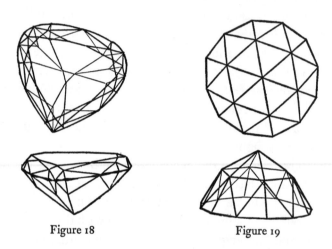

Figure 18   Figure 19

part been given some variation of a step cutting, but even in this there appears to be no set rule, and the details of the facetting are largely a matter of individual taste on the part of the lapidaries.

The *rose* cut or *rosette* enjoys a history more ancient, if not more honorable, than the brilliant cut. As far back as the early decades to the sixteenth century this form of cutting was in vogue for diamonds. It is said that several of the diamonds of the French crown were recut to a rose form by the order of Cardinal Mazarin, an association of names which led to the tradition that the rose cut was invented by the famous ecclesiastic.

Since the seventeenth century the rose cut has steadily given place in popularity before the increased luster of each succeeding modification of the brilliant cut, and it is now used only for very small cluster diamonds and for such deep colored stones as Bohemian garnet.

One of the earliest variations of the rose cut is the Holland rose, Figure 19. In its simplest and probably its oldest form this cutting consisted of only 12 facets above the flat base, arranged in two stepped rows of six each. The rose cut shown in the figure was probably derived from this, the primitive phase, by the addition of 12 facets around the base, which correspond to the corner facets of a brilliant cut. The six upper facets constitute the crown, and the 18 facets of the lower row are known as the cross facets. As applied to the diamond, much of the light which falls on the facets of the Holland rose in a direction normal to the base is returned to the eye above the base, but owing to the small number of reflections for each pencil of rays, the rainbow-like colors which constitute the chief charm of a brilliant cut are lacking.

The Brabant rose presents the same general arrangement of facets as the Holland rose, but differs from the latter in that the ring of cross facets is steeper and the crown lower. Optically this cutting is not nearly so efficient as the other forms of rose cut, most of the incident rays of light escaping through the base, a fact which probably accounts for its early lapse from popularity. This cutting apparently originated in Antwerp when that city was contending with Amsterdam as a diamond-cutting center, and represents an unsuccessful attempt to rival a characteristic Dutch cutting.

Both of the above rose cuts have been slightly varied; as, for instance, in the substitution of one instead of two facets in the double cut which takes off the corners of the base, giving to the cut 19 instead of 25 facets. Another variation carries the crown facets of the single cut to the base in a six or eight-sided pyramid, and double cuts each corner, with one facet carried half way up the edge and making the crown facets lozenge shaped. This is known as the cross rose.

The rose recoupee, a more elaborate variation of the Holland rose, is shown in Figure 20. This has twice the number of single

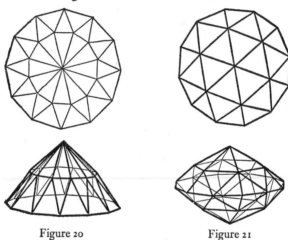

Figure 20   Figure 21

cut facets, that is, 24; and because the single cutting is more elaborate, only one double cut facet for each corner is given. This makes a cutting of 37 facets with a 12 sided base. From the point of view of effective brilliancy, the rose recoupee far exceeds the other cuttings of this class, the leakage through the base being relatively small, and in general the light is returned through the crown facets.

The double rose, Figure 21, is a variation hardly less classic than the Holland rose from which it was derived. It has the form of two Holland rose cuttings joined base to base, and is particularly appropriate for stones which are to be used as pendants or pendant eardrops. Set in a loop which clasps the girdle, it would seem that the brilliancy of this cutting, as applied to diamonds, has been somewhat overlooked; a study of the optics brings out the fact that it gives very effective reflections through the cross facets, and that these reflected rays would, in all probability, produce through their interference a desirable play of color.

So closely allied to the double rose as to almost constitute part

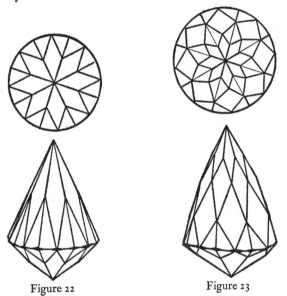

Figure 22   Figure 23

of the same variation are the numerous forms of *pendeloque* cutting.[1] These may be considered as double rose cuts of which the axis of one end has been drawn out to a very steep crown, while the other end is terminated by a rose of ordinary height of crown or by one with this height slightly depressed. The pendeloque shown in Figure 22 may be said to be formed by two roses recoupee, and represents a rather simple cutting in this style. For

[1] There appears to be a diversity of nomenclature in relation to this form of cutting, several authors mentioning it as a "briolette" or "briolette brilliant." In using the term "pendeloque" the present author follows the precedent of Dr. Max Bauer.

pendants of the semiprecious stones pendeloque cuttings are eminently adapted, and they are met with most frequently in the make of the quartz gems, rock crystal, amethyst, citrine and smoky quartz. The larger stones are given a more elaborate treatment, as in Figure 23, which was studied from a smoky quartz pendant. Still more elaborate variations are common in the treatment of this cutting, some of them running as high as 88 or more facets. Much latitude is also permissible with regard to the proportion of length to diameter, and the shorter forms when cut from relatively soft stones are usually bored through the axis to admit of their being strung.

From the pendeloque cutting it is but a short step to the beads and other cuttings intended to be strung. One of the most usual forms of round bead cut is the one shown in Figure 24, which was studied from an amethyst bead of 13¼ carats. This treatment of a facetted bead may be found in almost all the materials used for this purpose, particularly in amethyst and amber. That it is a very ancient and obvious method of facetting is evidenced by the beads of the Gallo-Roman Period.

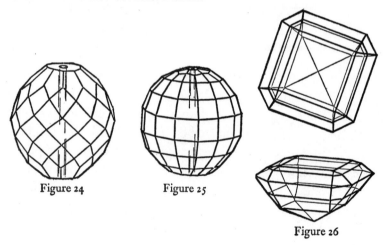

Figure 24   Figure 25

Figure 26

A much more unusual bead cutting is that shown in Figure 25, which might be termed a stepped bead. It was studied from one of a string of 29 superbly cut rock crystals and represents one from about the middle of the string which weighed about 15 carats. Some of the larger of these beads were cut with cross facets for the two terminating rows of facets, and, in at least one instance, one end of the axis was treated as in the figure, and the other facetted for two rows as in Figure 24.

Allied to these bead cuttings is the egg-shaped cutting given to the large blue topaz, illustrated in Chapter IX. The stone, which represents one of the finest examples of the lapidary's art, is cut with 444 facets of perfect regularity, and is so proportioned that it gives very effective brilliancy.

When we turn back to the beginning of the art of shaping gem minerals into forms adapted to jewelry settings, we find a perfectly obvious sequence in the development of these forms. It is a sequence which, in fact, adheres closely to the lines upon which a lapidary of the present day is trained in his art. First, we have the round or oval cabochon cuttings of Celtic, Byzantine and early French jewelry, often somewhat irregular in shape, the simplest and crudest efforts in the dawning art of fashioning stones to enrich the masterpieces of the medieval goldsmiths and silversmiths. With the development of richer design in jewelry there followed a steady progress in gem cutting, and with the call for stones of square and octagonal outline there began to be evolved cuttings with broad table facets flanked by narrow bevels to admit of the stones being gripped by the heavy settings. This early form of facetted cutting, which is essentially a primitive step cut, shows its influence in the presence of a table facet on early forms in the evolution of the brilliant cut (see Figures 3 and 4).

From such crude beginnings to the typical emerald cut (Figure

26) of the present day, the advance has been only along the lines of more complex and symmetrical facetting, produced with a view to making a stone of more elegance of outline, where the display of the color is the primary consideration. In this way the form of step cut shown in Figure 26 is very widely used for emeralds and is given proportions directly dependent on the depth of color in the stone to be cut.

A fairly recent practice in diamond cutting has adapted the step cut to the making of diamond gems of especially choice quality. When applied to diamond, however, the proportions of the step cut must be carefully studied with respect to the effective rays of light which are returned through the crown facets after total reflection within the stone.

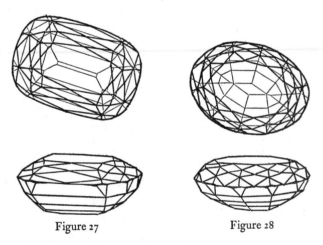

Figure 27   Figure 28

By far the most widely recognized derivatives from the step cut are those combination cuttings which use a brilliant or modified brilliant cut treatment for the crown facets and a stepped facetting for the pavilion end of the stone. One of these derivatives has been already discussed under variations of the brilliant cut, for the reason that it belonged more properly among the cuttings with round girdles than in the present group of cuttings, which include oval and oblong variants of the step cut, notably characterized by their complex multiplication of facets.

Cuttings of this kind are almost universally applied to large stones of the light colored gem minerals, such as amethyst, aquamarine, topaz, citrine, light colored tourmaline, peridot, smoky quartz, etc. In the example illustrated in Figure 27, which was studied from a blueish green aquamarine of 30½ carats weight, the brilliant cut treatment of the crown includes two rows of main facets instead of one, the large size of the stone necessitating an increase in the number of facets to give symmetry and surface brilliancy to the cutting.

Figure 28 also was studied from an aquamarine, in this instance a stone of 13½ carats. The oval shape is produced by the use of 10 instead of eight groups of facets, and, as in the former instance, the main facets are doubled in the crown and the stepped facets of the pavilion are accommodated to the oval girdle by single corner facets. The beauty of this stone has well repaid the lapidary for the labor of cutting 122 facets which constitute its make, and it may well be considered a masterpiece of well balanced and accurate gem cutting.

With larger stones the number of facets demanded by this cut may be increased almost indefinitely. Leopold Claremont illustrates[1] a very large oval aquamarine which is cut with 313 facets in the crown alone. But unless well proportioned and symmetrically distributed, the multiplication of facets in the combination step-brilliant cut tends only to detract the eye from the color, which constitutes the real beauty of the large semiprecious stones.

[1] "The Gem Cutter Craft," page 182.

Extremely simple are the tools and methods employed by the lapidary working in stones other than diamonds. A wheel or lap, a stick to hold the gem, a notched peg (seen behind his right hand), and his own consummate manual skill suffice him.

Photograph by Dr. Henry H. Russell

CEYLON GEM CUTTER AT WORK

The method of this native gem cutter reduces the implements of his craft to a minimum. The wheel which does the cutting is rotated by a kind of bow-string wrapped around a drum. The stone is held in his left hand.

Photograph from The American Gem and Pearl Company

POLISHING TOOLS

For polishing the parts of an intricate carving the craftsman uses a small gourd skin or ox-leather wheel. In the actual cutting of the design even smaller abrasive wheels and drills are employed.

The Cullinan diamond. The largest uncut diamond ever found, this stone weighed 3106 carats, or about a pound and a quarter. It was found in the Premier Mine No. 2, in Transvaal, South Africa.

Courtesy of American Museum of Natural History

A diamond crystal embedded in the "blue ground," characteristic of the South African diamond occurrence.

Courtesy of American Museum of Natural History

THE BIG HOLE AT KIMBERLY

Underwood & Underwood

CHAPTER V

"And right as the pearl of its own nature takes roundness, so the diamond, by virtue of God, takes squareness."
—TRAVELS OF SIR JOHN MANDEVILLE
(14th Century)

CHAPTER V

The Diamond

A s a gem mineral, diamond is in so many ways an unusual substance that we are fully justified in considering it as standing apart among the gems in a class by itself. To enumerate the points on which it may be considered unique, it is the hardest natural substance known, a property which, as we have seen, is responsible for a distinctive technique being employed in cutting and polishing it as compared with that used for other gem stones.

Diamond is composed of a single element, carbon. Thus it is chemically the simplest of all the gems.

Although colorless examples occur among almost all the mineral species that constitute the gem stones, these colorless varieties are held in little esteem *except in the case of diamond*. Colorless diamonds are in general esteemed the most desirable, and all estimates of value for them are consequently based on the degree to which they approach the standard of a perfectly colorless or "white" stone.

In the case of gem stones other than diamond, gems are obtained from a relatively rare gem variety of a fairly common mineral species. But there are no common diamonds; all transparent dia- monds are potentially gem stones.

Like almost every other activity that ministers to the comfort of man and gratifies his taste for the beautiful, the search for and retrieving of diamonds from the earth has had a history, in this case an ancient, interesting and romantic one. As far as we know, diamonds were first found in Central India, thus carrying out the tradition that very many of the precious and semiprecious stones originate in the Orient. Just how much of the sentiment which seems to be at the real bottom of the value of gems is linked with the romance and mysticism of the East is something for the psy- chologist to think about. The fact remains that diamonds, to- gether with other precious stones, take rank among the most valuable things to be found on our planet, not altogether because of their beauty—although this is great—nor exclusively by reason of their rarity, but on account of something more subtle, a lure which is more deeply seated in our being than any that can be estimated on a material basis.

The ancient diamond workings of India were scattered over quite a wide area, but the distributing center or mart was the town of Golconda, a name which has always been highly suggestive of opulence. As far back as that ancient epic, the Mahabharata, dia- monds have figured largely in the life and history of the Hindoos, and it was from India that they were introduced into Europe.

With the development of diamond cutting in Antwerp and Amsterdam in the fifteenth century, diamonds began to be more widely used by the Western nations. Such travellers as Jean Bap- tiste Tavernier (1665) brought back from the East stories of the magnificence of the diamonds owned by Oriental potentates, and so the use of them among people of wealth and power was stimu- lated. But the prestige of the Orient as a diamond producing section of the world has steadily waned, so that at present comparatively few stones come from those once famous fields. The diamond pits and diggings which occurred in sandstone or conglomerate, or among the sands and gravels of old river beds, have become so exhausted of their former richness that today one would have to search far and wide among jewelers to find an Indian diamond.

In 1725 diamonds were discovered in Brazil. This new field, which comprised a relatively small district within the states of Bahia, Minas Geraes, Goyaz and Matto Grasso, for a time yielded so many diamonds that there was grave danger of depreciation in their value. This danger was, however, overcome by the action of the Portuguese government, which imposed heavy duties on diamonds and otherwise rendered the working of the mines unprofitable except at high prices.

The Brazilian diamonds, like those of India, occurred in gravels and conglomerates, and much of the later mining operations to recover them have taken the form of dredging the river beds and washing down the gravel deposits by water under pressure (hydraulic mining).

For a century and a half Brazil enjoyed the distinction of furnishing most of the world's supply of these precious stones, so that the diamonds that have come down to us as heirlooms from the last century are for the most part Brazilian stones, and for purity of color there are none better to be found the world over. The development of diamond fields moves with the explorer, the prospector and the pioneer. And so it was that in 1867 an enterprising small boy, the son of a Boer farmer living on the banks of the Vaal River in South Africa, picked up what seemed to him to be a pebble, but was in reality a large diamond. After many adventures, this now historic pebble was sold in Paris for $2,500, and so marked the beginning of a new era in the history of diamond seeking. For the next 30 years the great South African diamond fields yielded the enormous total of something like seven and one half tons of rough stones, which were approximately valued at $450,-000,000 after cutting. Today South Africa furnishes 98 percent of the rapidly increasing production of the world in diamonds.

The South African diamond discovery was made in what are now termed the "river diggings" located along the course of the Vaal River northwest of Kimberley, and so situated that the influx of miners travelling in from Delagoa Bay or Durban must, to reach their destination, have had to pass almost directly over the richer deposits of Kimberley. It is consequently not at all to be wondered at that the discovery of the famous diamond pipe at Kimberley should have followed close upon the heels of the development of the Vaal River deposits, and that the supremacy of South Africa as a diamond producing country should thus be firmly established. Unlike the Vaal diggings, which are gravel deposits in the bed and near the banks of the river, the great diamond workings of Kimberley are situated in vast volcanic tubes or pipes, through which in the far remote past molten rock was forced up from the earth's interior through overlying layers of shales, conglomerates and gneisses. The filling of these volcanic pipes consists of a stiff volcanic tuff or breccia known as the "blue ground," which in its upper layers to a depth of 50 to 60 feet has yielded to decomposition, forming a somewhat loose friable, light colored mass called the "yellow ground." The rock forming the walls of the pipe is known as the "reef." It is in the blue ground and the overlying yellow ground that the diamonds occur, and their mining history has no doubt been much influenced by the fact that the cheapest and easiest mining was encountered by the pioneers, the owners and workers of small claims, in the upper

layers of the yellow ground, and not in the stiffer and more re-
fractory blue ground. From the nature of the case, however, the
depth to which it was possible to excavate the Kimberley pipe
before the difficulties engendered by the frequent falling in of
the sides of the reef became acute, was limited. This stage of development was reached comparatively early in the history of the
field, and in 1889, after a colossal battle with his financial rival,
Barnett Isaacs, otherwise known as "Barnato," Cecil Rhodes suc-
ceeded in obtaining control of the separate small claims and
amalgamated them into a huge corporation. The subsequent mining operation took the form of shafts sunk through the reef, from
which the diamond bearing blue ground was reached by side
tunnels, and the resources of the deposit rendered available for a
practically indefinite period.

The blue ground as it comes from the mine is broken up and
spread out on "floors" or open stretches of veldt for periods ranging from six months to two years, in order that the rain and other
atmospheric agencies may act upon it. In this way the blue ground
is transformed by weathering into yellow ground and can be run
through a series of washing devices, the object of which is to
separate out the loose pebbles, among which are the diamonds. By
a comparatively recent invention the necessity of handling the
diamonds in separating them from the other pebbles has been
obviated. This device consists of a number of inclined tables, over
which the water from the washers flows, carrying with it and
depositing on the tables the pebbles. The tables, to which a slight
shaking motion is imparted, are covered with grease, a substance
which has the property of attaching to itself the diamonds, while
the pebbles of other minerals pass freely over the table and are
caught in a trough at the bottom of the device. The grease is
from time to time scraped from the tables, and the diamonds are

recovered from it.

Besides the diamond fields in the vicinity of Kimberley and the Vaal River group, Africa must be credited with another group of mines, those of Southwest Africa. Although of relatively less importance than its neighbors, the Southwest African field in one year, just prior to the World War, produced over $4,000,000 in diamonds. Within recent years a diamond field in the southern part of the Belgian Congo has attained a considerable importance. The African diamonds in general do not quite equal those of Brazil in the purity of the blue white color which is the test of a fine stone. They average a higher percentage of stones that are classed as off color, that is, slightly yellowish in tint. It would seem as though nature balanced the great quantity of the African yield by a slight falling off in fineness of quality.

Australia produces diamonds on a rather small scale, the stones occurring near Bathurst and Madgee in New South Wales. Australian stones are said to resemble those from Brazil. In Borneo a few diamonds are mined near the west coast of the island. Both the Australian and the Borneo diamonds are harder than those from other countries, a considerable distinction when we recall that diamonds are by far the hardest of all natural substances.

There is also a small but promising patch of diamond bearing rock near Murfreesboro in Arkansas, which proves that the United States were not altogether left out when nature scattered diamonds over the world. The latest find of diamonds has been in British Guiana, where a remote but what seems to be a promising field exists. Should this prove to be an important source of diamonds, this hemisphere may again challenge Africa as a diamond producer. Like almost all other minerals diamonds are found in nature in crystals which, when undistorted by the forces which have influenced their formation, are singularly regular in shape and which are distinctive. Anyone who has seen and studied a series of uncut diamonds will be enabled thereafter to recognize readily diamond crystals from among scores of others. To such an extent is this true that in times past, and in all the diamond fields of the world, natives of no education and low intelligence have been successfully employed to sort diamonds by hand from masses of pebbles of all shapes and consisting of many minerals.

The simplest form of a diamond crystal is, as we have seen in the chapter on how diamonds are cut and polished, an octahedron, a geometrical solid having eight triangular faces. Complex modifications of the simple octahedron by other crystal forms often operate to produce in diamond crystals a multiplicity of small crystal faces, which give to them the resemblance of having rounded instead of flat sides. With this effect of roundness, characteristic of many diamonds in the rough, there will always be found an equally characteristic surface luster, which has been described as resembling a coating of oil.

Aside from the unusual colors, such as blue, red, green and canary yellow, which, in rare instances when they are present, very much increase the value of diamonds, the standard of perfection for this precious gem is pure white. Divergence from this standard is mainly in the direction of yellow and brownish stones, the coloring matter having been assumed to be extremely minute quantities of iron oxide. Since even a very slight shading of yellow is sufficient to lower materially the value of a diamond, a rigorous conformity to a number of standard grades of color is in effect among sorters and merchants of diamond, which grades represent differences so slight that only long training and experience can detect them. It is customary for those who judge and appraise diamonds to dim the brilliancy of the stone by breathing on it, after which the true color or lack of it is more easily judged.

CHAPTER VI

"The greatest value among the objects of human property, not merely among precious stones, is due to the adamas (diamond), for a long time known only to kings and even to very few of these."
—PLINY, HISTORIA NATURALIS (A.D. 77)

CHAPTER VI

Famous Diamonds of the World

J UST AS "Golconda" has become synonymous with a source of fabulous wealth, so the possession of large and fine diamonds has always carried with it the distinction attached to abundant riches. Even before recorded history these fragments of concentrated wealth and power have moved men to war and murder, acquisitiveness and villainy. It is, then, far from surprising that the role of large and valuable diamonds in the shaping of history should be an important and a romantic one, and that the accounts of their careers should be well worth the telling.

Many of these famous stones have been said to have brought ill luck to those who, from time to time, have been the possessors of them. This legend of ill luck which has so often been attributed to objects of rarity has its root in the fact that misfortune is much more common in human experience than in the ownership of, let us say, a valuable diamond. A person whose ill fortune seems to exceed that of his neighbor will search for something which he has and his neighbor has not, on which to place the blame; and a large blue diamond or a specially fine opal may easily be made responsible for the more usual occurrence.

The value of diamonds, contrary to popular opinion, does not increase in direct proportion to the size, or, rather, the weight of the stones. An old rule, much in use during the last century, makes the value increase in proportion to the square of the weight. According to this rule a diamond weighing two carats would be worth four times, and not twice, the value of a one carat stone of the same quality. In the same way a three carat diamond would have a value of nine times that of a one carat standard. This rule held, in general, while relatively low values of small stones prevailed, and many of the sales of famous diamonds that were recorded fifty or one hundred years ago were made on this basis.

With the growing demand for diamonds weighing from one to five carats, however, the standard of value for a one carat brilliant-cut stone has vastly increased, and with this increase has come a very material modification of the old rule for estimating diamond values. One may almost say that the present value of a large stone depends entirely on its marketability, which is equivalent to saying that a diamond dealer appraises a large stone at a price that he considers his prospective buyer is willing to pay for it.

As we have read in the previous chapter, the world's supply of diamonds previous to the eighteenth century was furnished entirely by the Indian mines. It is therefore obvious that the large stones having the most ancient and consequently the most romantic history first saw the light of day in that country of adventure and intrigue.

Foremost among the world's gems in the matter of romantic history is the diamond known as the Koh-i-nor. The authentic history of this famous stone begins very early in the fourteenth century, when it figured as a portion of the treasure taken from the reigning Rajah of Malwar, whose kingdom was conquered by a neighboring prince. Previous to this time it had been in the possession of the rulers of Malwar for many generations, and there is a tradition that it was found in the Godavary River four or five thousand years ago, and that it was worn by one of the heroes of that celebrated Hindoo epic, the Mahabharata.

With the Mogul conquest of India in 1526, the Koh-i-nor passed into the possession of the Mogul rulers, and it remained in the treasury at Delhi until, in 1739, the rulership of India again changed hands and India's "stone of destiny" became the property of Nadir Shah, the Persian conqueror. During the Mogul Empire the Koh-i-nor is said to have been set in one of the eyes of the celebrated "Peacock Throne." When Nadir Shah first saw the size and beauty of this peerless gem, which in its native cutting weighed 186 carats, he exclaimed "Kohinor!" (Mountain of Light).

Upon the transfer of the Koh-i-nor from India to Persia its career in that land of assassination and intrigue was marked by a long succession of murders, tortures and imprisonments, the almost invariable lot of its unfortunate owners. After many thrilling adventures it became the spoil of Runjit Singh, the Lion of the Punjab, who had it set in a bracelet which graced his arm on state occasions. After the death of Runjit Singh, it remained in the Punjab treasury at Lahore until that portion of India was annexed by the British Government in 1849. Following its destiny, the Koh-i-nor now became the property of the conquering sovereign, and was officially presented to Queen Victoria, who caused it to be recut, reducing its weight from 186 carats to nearly 109 metric carats. Inasmuch as the Koh-i-nor, as far as is known, never changed hands through purchase, it is next to impossible to form any estimate of its value. The work of recutting it is said to have cost $40,000, a very doubtful improvement, since in its present form much of the stone's historical significance is lost.

Just as the Koh-i-nor is involved in the old history of India, so is the diamond known as the Regent or Pitt mingled with the modern history of France. This historic gem was discovered in 1701 in the diamond mines at Partial, about 150 miles from Golconda in Central India. When found by a native mine laborer, it weighed 410 carats, by far too bulky an object to be concealed upon the person. The finder, however, solved the difficulty of its concealment by cutting his leg and hiding the diamond in the folds of cloth with which he bandaged his wound. He made his way to the coast, and realizing the danger of being found with a stolen diamond, he bartered his loot in exchange for "a free passage to a distant land." The English skipper who made this bargain with him must have placed a sinister interpretation on the terms of the contract, for the poor slave was thrown to the sharks and the diamond sold to a Parsee merchant for $5,000. The Parsee merchant was evidently a clever financier, for he resold the diamond to Sir Thomas Pitt, Governor of Fort St. George at Madras, for about $100,000. Although this transaction was a perfectly honorable one on the part of Sir Thomas Pitt, the implications and criticism which met him upon his return to England caused him to lose no time in realizing a profit on the Pitt diamond, as it was now named. Accordingly, after a reduction in weight from 410 carats in the rough to a brilliant of 143 carats through cutting, we find the Pitt diamond sold in 1717 to the Duke of Orleans, Regent of France, who bought it for the French crown jewels for over $600,000.

This famous stone, now called the Regent diamond, remained

among the crown jewels of France until the fateful year 1792, when amid the disturbance of the Revolution, it was stolen with other crown jewels from the Garde-meuble. The thieves, however, found such difficulty in disposing of the well-known diamond that it was abandoned and was found some weeks later in a ditch in the Champs-Elysées.

Having suffered no loss of value through its adventures, the Regent returned to its high rank as the first jewel of France, and a year or so later it was pledged by the Republican Government to Holland for money with which expenses of the Napoleonic wars were met. Redeemed by Napoleon, it was mounted in the hilt of his state sword. It now rests, the pride of a great nation, in the Galerie d'Apollon of the Louvre.

Among the known historical diamonds the sole example that has retained its original East Indian cutting is the stone now known as the Orloff. When first brought to notice, this gem formed one of the eyes of the statue of Brahma in a temple at Trichinopoli, in Mysore, southern India. Early in the eighteenth century it was seen there by a French soldier, who, having assumed the character of a native devotee and having been made guardian of the temple, stole the idol's eye and escaped with it to Madras. Here he sold his plunder to an English sea captain for $10,000, who in turn disposed of it to a London gem dealer for $60,000. After several subsequent changes of ownership it was sold in Amsterdam to Prince Orloff of the Russian Court for a sum that was said to have reached the high figure for that period, $450,000. The Prince, hoping to regain the lost favor of Catherine II, presented the Orloff diamond to the Crown of Russia, where it has remained set in the royal scepter to this day. It weighs close to 195 carats, and is one of the treasures of the Union of Soviet

Socialist Republics.

The largest of cut Indian diamonds is indeed a stone of mystery. Seen by that famous traveler, Jean Baptiste Tavernier, in 1665, the Great Mogul, as he named this great diamond of the Mogul Court treasure, weighed 279 carats. The sketch of the Great Mogul as brought back by Tavernier is very like the Orloff in cut.

Shortly after Tavernier's visit the Great Mogul was lost from sight. In the opinion of Dr. Fersman, the noted Russian gem expert, the Orloff and the Great Mogul are identical. This authority explains the apparent discrepancy in weight between the two stones by assuming a mistake on the part of Tavernier in estimating the weight of the Indian standard of diamond weight, the *rati,* in terms of European diamond weights.

No diamond, not even the fateful Koh-i-nor, can claim a more romantic past in fact and fable than the almond shaped stone, weighing only 53 carats, and known to fame as the Sancy diamond. The Sancy has been said by some writers to have been identical with that cut by Louis de Berquem for Charles the Bold, and worn by him at the disastrous battle of Nancy, where in 1477 the power of Burgundy went down, carrying its duke with it. The Duke's diamond was taken from his dead body by a Swiss soldier, and at this point a gap occurs in its history.

A diamond of the same shape and approximate weight was brought to France from the East by Nicholas Harlai, Seigneur de Sancy, about the year 1570, de Sancy being at that time French Ambassador to the Ottoman Court. From this point the varied history of the Sancy diamond is a matter of record. In the reign of Henry IV de Sancy was minister of finance and offered his diamond as a pledge to his sovereign, who wished to borrow money for an increase of his army. The jewel was sent by a trusted messenger, who, however, never arrived, since he was waylaid, murdered and robbed. But not of the Sancy diamond. The faithful servant swallowed the gem before he fell under the knives of the bandits, and his master, knowing something of his devotion, recovered it from his stomach.

At some time between 1590 and 1600 the Sancy diamond was sold to Queen Elizabeth of England. It remained among the English crown jewels until the widow of Charles I presented it to the Earl of Worcester. By purchase or gift it again came back to the English crown jewels, for we find it among them in the reign of James II, who sold it to Louis XIV about the year 1695 for $625,000.

It disappeared temporarily when the Garde-meuble was robbed in 1792, but reappeared in 1828 when Prince Demidoff of Russia purchased it from a French dealer for $100,000. During the nineteenth century it was sold several times for varying sums. According to authentic sources its last purchaser was the Maharajah of Patiala.

The steely blue stone known as the Hope Blue is the largest and most celebrated among the colored diamonds. Although this stone is known in its present form only since 1830, several excellent authorities agree that its history antedates that year.

When Tavernier returned from his earlier voyage to India in 1642, he brought with him a blue diamond weighing 67 carats cut as a drop pointed at one end, and somewhat resembling the Sancy in cut. This stone was sold to Louis XIV in 1668 and met the fate of the other crown jewels in 1792 when the French treasury was robbed. But unlike most of the other spoils of the most sensational gem robbery of history, it was never seen again.

In 1830 the present blue diamond weighing 44 carats appeared in London and was sold to Sir Thomas Hope for $90,000; and at about this time a smaller blue diamond also appeared on the market. A theory that has been advanced by the late E. W. Streeter makes the Hope Blue diamond the larger of two portions of Tavernier's stone after the point of the drop had been cut from it. This theory, which has several supporters among modern gem writers, gathers force from the fact that one side of the oblong brilliant is straighter than the opposite side. The Hope Blue was sold at a Paris auction in 1909, and in 1911 was purchased by the late Mr. Edward McLean of Washington for $300,000.

The greatest diamond that has yet been found is also the most modern of all world-famous gems. In January, 1905, a fragment of diamond crystal weighing 3106 metric carats was found in the Premier Mine, 20 miles northwest of Pretoria in the Transvaal, a province of South Africa. This huge stone was named the Cullinan in honor of Sir T. M. Cullinan, President of the Premier Diamond Mining Company. It was purchased by the Transvaal Government for a sum variously stated as $750,000 and $800,000 and presented as a crown jewel to King Edward VII on his birthday, November 9, 1907.

The famous firm of I. J. Asscher and Company of Amsterdam, to whom was entrusted the all important task of cutting it into the most effective brilliants, found it necessary to cleave it in three to avoid a flaw in the center. From these thirds the two greatest known cut diamonds were obtained, a pendeloque, or pendant-cut brilliant, weighing 530 carats, and a square brilliant, weighing 317 carats. The larger of these, the world's largest cut diamond, was called the Cullinan No. 1, and was set in the scepter of the

British regalia. The Cullinan No. 2 was set in the crown. In addition to these the Cullinan diamond furnished seven other major stones, varying in weight from 94 to 4⅓ carats, all of which are among the crown jewels of Great Britain.

When George V came to the throne, one of his first acts concerned the change of name of the famous Cullinan No. 1 diamond to the "Star of Africa." At that time he gave as his reason for this change that in his opinion a jewel that belonged to the people of the British Empire should bear the name of a part of Great Britain, rather than that of a private individual. And this opinion would seem to be the finest thing that any King has ever said about any diamond.

THE STAR OF AFRICA

Courtesy of Harry Winston

Upper left–Koh-i-nor (original cutting). *Upper right*–Koh-i-nor (recut). *Lower left*–Great Mogul. *Lower right*–Orloff.

Top–Hope Blue.
Lower left–Sancy.
Lower right–Regent or Pitt.

A gem crystal of emerald surrounded by the light gray limestone matrix which accompanies this precious stone, in the mines at Muso, Colombia.

Courtesy of American Museum of Natural History

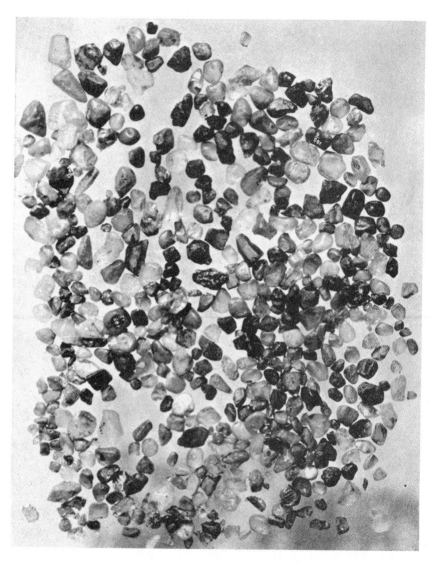

A handful of gem gravel from Ceylon. Rubies, sapphires, as well as some of the fancy corundum gem colors, glow among these pebbles from alluvial gravel beds.

CHAPTER VII

"The sapphire is a precious stone and is blue in color most like to heaven in fair weather and clear, and is best among precious stones and most apt and able to fingers of kings."
—BARTHOLOMEW ANGELICUS (13th Century)

CHAPTER VII

Precious Stones
Other Than Diamonds

W HEN we endeavor to formulate a division between the precious and the semiprecious gem stones, as one of definite classification, we are immediately faced by several facts which complicate the issue and render what would seem a relatively simple matter both difficult and elusive.

In the first place, we have the instance of a gem mineral, such as beryl, furnishing both a precious stone, the emerald, and several semiprecious stones, aquamarine, golden beryl and morganite.

Again, gem values, which are our only standard of comparison, are very much influenced by a shifting and capricious fashion, so that a gem stone that today commands a price per carat which places it in the precious stone class, may in ten years dwindle in value to a point where it becomes a semiprecious gem. And of course the process may be reversed, as when a popular demand for a gem of a certain color sets a precious stone value on a gem formerly ranked as semiprecious.

Today the precious stones include diamond, ruby, sapphire,

and emerald, although, strictly on a basis of value, such gems as alexandrite and opal should also be classed as precious.

The gem varieties of the mineral corundum, which for convenience we are considering under the heading of the corundum gems, include two which we have named in the preceding paragraph: a deep red corundum, known as the ruby; and a fine rich blue corundum, known as the sapphire. It is remarkable that this mineral species is the only one that furnishes us with *two* precious stones of such pronounced and magnificent color.

In chemical composition corundum is a sesquioxide of aluminium, and when free from the smallest trace of other metallic oxides, its crystals are absolutely colorless. The wide range of color displayed by its gem varieties is entirely due to small quantities, rarely more than one percent, of such coloring agents as chromic oxide, titanic oxide and ferric oxide. For instance, we have every reason to suppose that the splendid red color that distinguishes the ruby from all other gems is due to a very small amount of chromic oxide, and that the deep blue of sapphire is produced by titanic oxide. Corundum ranks next after diamond in hardness, a quality which has always made the corundum gems particularly desirable as stones for ring settings.

RUBY

Although found in other parts of the world, the corundum gems come essentially from the Oriental countries. For rubies of the true *pigeon blood* quality (see color plate frontispiece), which is a shade of red with a slight admixture of purple, and is ranked as the highest standard of color, we must go to Mogok in Upper Burma. At these famous mines, which are of great antiquity, the rubies occur in a granular limestone that forms the sides of the hills. But, since these limestone outcrops have been eroded by weathering through countless ages, a far more prolific source of rubies is furnished by the alluvial deposits of clay and gravel that have been washed down into the adjacent river beds. A handful of pebbles from these river gravels shows all the colors of the rainbow, because among them are to be found not only fragments of the many colored corundum gems, but also spinels and tourmalines.

Generation after generation of natives have sorted these gravels, being rewarded with an occasional deep colored ruby. Up to a generation ago the native miners were compelled to give up all stones over a certain weight to the local ruler, whose treasury is said to have contained in consequence some very remarkable rubies. Southward from Mogok, about 400 miles as the crow flies, is the famous Hill of Precious Stones, near Bangkok in Siam, where rubies of a rather darker color than those from Burma occur under somewhat similar conditions. A good judge of rubies can detect the slight shade of color that distinguishes the Burmese stones from those of Siam, and since the former are considered the choicest in color they command a higher price per carat.

A celebrated ruby mine is situated near Kabul in Afghanistan and is known as the Amir's mine.

SAPPHIRE

The standard color for a sapphire is a cornflower blue (see color plate frontispiece), deep enough to show richness of tint by daylight, but light enough to retain its color by artificial light. Stones of this quality of color come from the Zanskar range of the Himalayas, in Kashmir, a region that has produced a number of large and fine gems. The Hill of Precious Stones in Siam is also noted for the splendid sapphires that have been mined there.

The dry water courses and stream bottoms of Central and

Southern Ceylon are famous for the gem gravels, washed down from the gneiss and limestone rocks of higher elevation. When sorted, much of this gem gravel consists of corundum gems, notably sapphires of varying degree of depth of color.

During the latter years of the last century a limited production of sapphires was obtained from near Helena, Montana, some of which were of fine color. The best of these stones were taken from workings in the gneiss rock, the alluvial gravels, although present, as in Ceylon, yielding stones of relatively light and poor color. About the same period, or earlier, some rubies of fair quality were found in North Carolina.

Australian sapphires, which come from Anakie in Queensland, are generally considered to be too deep in color to stand comparison with the best Kashmiri, Siamese or Ceylonese stones.

Although rubies and sapphires are best known among the corundum gems, red and blue by no means exhaust the wide range of their color. A golden yellow occurring notably at the Ceylon localities completes the series of primary colors, and is often referred to as "Oriental topaz."

The color distribution in all corundum gems is somewhat uneven, lying in bands parallel to the six-sided crystals which characterize corundum. Nor is the color always uniform in tint. In many instances successive bands of red and blue produce the effect of various shades of purple, violet and wisteria. In the same manner alternate bandings of blue and yellow give a mass effect of green, and red and yellow alternate to produce a somewhat rare shade of orange. In general, with the exception of the deep purple gems, sometimes referred to as "Oriental amethysts," these mixed colors are light in quality, and such stones are known among jewelers as "fancy sapphires."

The hexagonal or six-sided symmetry of corundum crystals is

responsible in certain gem varieties for a curious and beautiful effect which is known as asterism. Such gem crystals contain minute hollow tubes arranged with great regularity at angles of 60 degrees and in layers at right angles to the vertical axis of the crystal. When cut *en cabochon,* so that the rounded dome arches over these layers of cavities, stones of this kind reflect the light from the *interior* as a six-rayed star and are consequently termed star rubies and star sapphires. Star stones are never quite clear because of the presence of the hollow cavities, but are always more or less milky in aspect (see color plate frontispiece).

So many factors enter into the value of rubies and sapphires that it is very difficult to state even an approximate relative scale of values. A fine sapphire of the best color should command about the same value, carat for carat, as a fine diamond. On the same basis of comparison a pigeon blood ruby should be worth, carat for carat, from two to two and a half times as much as a standard diamond. Fancy sapphires are valued as semiprecious stones and compare in value with topazes or aquamarines. Star rubies are rarer than star sapphires and command higher prices, but neither variety approaches in value the best qualities of rubies and sapphires..

Because corundum is a relatively simple mineral in its chemical composition, being only an oxide of aluminium, its gem varieties have been very successfully reproduced artificially. This has been done by fusing the aluminium sesquioxide, to which has been added the proper proportion of coloring oxides to give the red or blue color, in the flame of an inverted oxyhydrogen blowpipe. In this process pure alumina mixed with the coloring oxide, both in the state of finely divided powder, falls into the combustion chamber, and there is built up into a little knob that looks like a colored glass, but is in reality an artificial ruby or sapphire. The artificial "boules" of red or blue alumina possess all the physical properties of natural rubies or sapphires. They have the hardness, the specific gravity, and even the optical properties of natural gems. Certain microscopic imperfections in the form of concentric rings of minute bubbles alone supply a means of distinguishing synthetic sapphires and rubies from natural stones.

EMERALD

The grass green variety of the mineral beryl, which since the days of Pliny has been called emerald (see color plate frontispiece), is today the supreme high point in gem values, having by reason of popular mode, which demands green rather than red stones, outranked even the ruby in this respect. The source of this color is said to be very small percentages of chromic oxides present in the silicate of aluminium and beryllium, which compose all the stones belonging to the beryl mineralogical family. Crystals of beryl occur in six-sided prisms whose ends are terminated either by single planes at right angles to the prism edges or by flat six-sided pyramids or by a combination of both of these modifications. In hardness the beryl gems, which include the emerald, are somewhat softer than rubies and sapphires, approaching dangerously near the limit at which a facetted gem stone may be used in ring mounts without showing undue wear on the edges.

Queen Cleopatra had an emerald mine that is still in existence near the shore of the Red Sea in Upper Egypt, although no emeralds are found there at present. It was perhaps from this place that the celebrated emerald through which Nero viewed the gladiatorial games came, and no doubt many of the gems of the ancient world are traceable to this source.

Emeralds have long been the glory of the Russian crown jew-

els. Their deep rich greens appealed to the almost barbaric love
of splendor that underlies Russian taste, and they were, moreover, to be found in Russian territory, on the Asiatic side of the
Ural Mountains near Ekaterinburg.

Both Egyptian and Russian emeralds occur in micaceous schists
and gneisses, the gem crystals in general exhibiting flaws and
"feathers" which materially detract from the value of the cut
stones. A similar schist-like rock at Habachtal, in the Salzburg
Alps, has produced a small amount of inferior emeralds. Also the
micaceous gneiss of North Carolina has furnished material from
which a few small stones have been cut. The great source of
emeralds of our own day is the now famous mine in the vicinity
of Muso in the republic of Colombia. The story of South American emeralds is a romantic one. When the Spaniards conquered
Peru and took from the Incas all their treasured wealth, they
found an immense number of emeralds, some of almost incredible
size, in the temples and on the persons of the conquered natives.
Thus was Europe soon flooded with what were then called
Spanish or Peruvian emeralds, although none of them came originally either from Spain or Peru. But neither persecution nor
torture could induce the unfortunate Incas to reveal the source
of their wealth of green stones, and it was only by accident that
in 1558 one of the native emerald mines was found near Muso
in Colombia. The natives had destroyed all traces of the others,
and the thick, impenetrable, tropical jungle had swallowed them
up. The Muso mine has been producing emeralds periodically
ever since, and in quality of color and freedom from imperfections they are far superior to stones from other sources. About
three decades ago another of the lost emerald mines of the Incas
was rediscovered at Sonondoco, not far from Muso. The stones
from this locality are said to be of not so fine a quality as those

from the latter mine. At Muso, as well as at Sonondoco, the emeralds occur in a crystalline limestone.

AQUAMARINE

Although ranking as first among the beryl gems, emerald is by no means the only gem stone to be found among the varieties of beryl. As many of us know, beryl is a rather common rock-forming silicate, and there are quite a number of kinds of beryl which are also cut for gem stones, and which are, as we might say, poor relations of the emerald.

One of the most beautiful of these is aquamarine. Its name describes it quite accurately—sea water. Have you ever stood near the bow of a moving vessel and watched the lovely green plume slide away from almost under your feet? That is the color of aquamarine. Sometimes there is more blue than green in the tint of this gem, as in the instance of some of the Brazilian stones, which are frankly and superbly blue (see color plate frontispiece), but for the most part, aquamarines range between greenish blue and blueish green. The color may be due to oxides of some of the alkaline earths and iron.

GOLDEN BERYL AND MORGANITE

Golden beryl is another beryl gem, in this instance of various shades of yellow, and the name morganite (in honor of the late J. P. Morgan) has been given to a beryl of a beautiful rose pink color. Aquamarines and golden beryls may be said to come from all over the globe, and that is the reason why these beryls are semiprecious and not precious stones.

From Russia on both sides of the Ural Mountains are obtained aquamarines of fine sea green colors. Blueish green and blue stones are found in Minas Novas and Minas Geraes, Brazil, as well as in Ceylon. Maine and North Carolina also have produced some finely colored aquamarines.

Golden beryls may be said to come in general from the same localities that are productive of aquamarines, and the finest morganite is found with other semiprecious beryls in Madagascar.

As to relative value, an emerald of the finest quality is worth from three and one half to four times the value of a diamond of highest grade, carat for carat.

Emeralds are almost universally cut in the form shown on page 60, with a square or rectangular girdle, depending on the proportions of the stone, and with the corners of the square or rectangle cut off as shown in the figure.

Aquamarines, because of the fact that they usually furnish large stones, are commonly made in a combination cut such as is shown in the two examples on page 62.

CHAPTER VIII

"... all the turf was rich in plots that looked
Each like a garnet or a turkis in it"
—GERAINT AND ENID,
TENNYSON

CHAPTER VIII

The Semiprecious Stones

BECAUSE oxygen and silicon are the commonest ingredients in the substance of the earth's crust, it follows that the great division of the silicate minerals, whose chemical constitution involves these two elements, should include in its comprehensive scope all of the common rock-forming minerals. It is indeed a dull witted and unobserving boy scout that can not show, as the result of his hike, a garnet or a tourmaline. Dull, commonplace affairs these are, just the stuff from which rocks are made, and yet capable under the right conditions of becoming deep colored and transparent. This, of course, is equivalent to saying that every common rock forming silicate may number among its varieties a gem stone, or putting it in a different way, any of the semiprecious stones is only a special sort of a common mineral having the attributes that go to make a gem. And inasmuch as there are often many kinds of a single common mineral, it follows that there may also be a number of gem varieties of such a mineral, each one having a somewhat different color, just as we found that there were red and blue and purple and yellow corundums.

TOPAZ

Topaz, which next to aquamarine is the best known semiprecious gem mineral, is a good example of a rock forming silicate that owes its origin to rather unusual conditions operating when the rock was in process of formation. Crystals of topaz are usually found in openings or cavities in fire-formed rocks and were formed by the action of hot acid vapors rich in fluorine upon the aluminium silicates that were largely present in the feldspars of these rocks. As a consequence of this method of formation, topaz is, as we would expect, a fluosilicate of aluminium. It is one of the hardest of the semi-precious stones, slightly exceeding in this respect the beryl gems, and much favored during the last century as a ring stone.

Much popular lack of information exists regarding the color of the topaz gems, and this is directly traceable to the comfortable fallacy of "one gem, one color." This is the first wrong idea of which we should rid ourselves in considering the semiprecious stones, because we have not, as in the case of the corundum gems and of the beryl gems, well known separate names for the different colors.

The best known and most popular color among gem varieties of topaz is a fine, lively yellow, much resembling the color of sherry wine (see color plate frontispiece). Stones cut from this tawny yellow variety are known among jewelers as *precious topaz*, and should not be confused with the *Oriental topaz*, which, as we saw in the last chapter, is a yellow kind of corundum, or with the smoky yellow, dull quartz gems that are often sold as "topaz."

Most of the wine yellow topaz of the finest color comes from Brazil, the three principal localities being Ouro Preto, Villa Rica and Minas Novas, all in the State of Minas Geraes. Ouro Preto is particularly noted for stones of a fine orange color. Stones of a lighter yellow are found among the gem gravels of Ceylon, having resulted, like other of the gem stones of these gravels, from the breaking down of the granite rocks in which they were formed.

Light green and light blue gem topaz crystals, to the eye closely resembling aquamarine in every respect except crystal form, have been found in Russia on both sides of the Ural Mountains and in Transbaikal, Siberia. Light, watery blue gem stones of considerable size have also been found in Japan, at Omi and Otami Yama.

Colorless topaz is even more common than the blueish variety and comes from the Ceylon and Russian localities, as well as from Japan, Mexico, Germany and several localities in the United States.

A rather rare and very attractive color is the reddish violet that characterizes the small gem crystals from Troisk, Government of Orenburg, Southeastern Russia. Unfortunately stones cut from crystals of this variety are very small, and consequently its use as a gem stone is practically negligible. Pink stones closely resembling the natural ones from Southeast Russia are produced artificially by subjecting the deep yellow topaz from Brazil to a slow and careful heating. Such "pinked" stones retain their color very well and are highly attractive, their popularity seemingly being proof against the menace of their artificiality.

Among the bewildering array of color presented by the topaz gems, the novice in gem determination may well ask how these are to be distinguished from many other species of more or less similar color value. Of course, in the case of a gem crystal the problem is very simple; a crystal of topaz, with its rhombic prism and twofold symmetry in termination, is not easily confused with one of corundum, or beryl, or quartz, even if we had not the added guide of the easy cleavage of topaz to help us by providing smooth, glistening surfaces where breaks occur. But with cut stones the problem is more difficult, and it is here that we must resort to the specific gravity, or relative weight, discussed in the introductory chapter. The specific gravity of topaz is practically constant and varies very little from 3.53, whatever may be the variety with which we are dealing. Yellow stones that might be mistaken for yellow topaz with their respective specific gravities are:—

Corundum (fancy sapphire)	4.03
Quartz (citrine or Spanish topaz)	2.66
Zircon	4.20

To distinguish blueish topaz from blueish aquamarine, we are guided by quite as clearly marked a difference in relative weight, since the beryl gems all have a specific gravity of 2.74.

And finally a pinked topaz, which might be confused with pink sapphire, spinel, the rubellite variety of tourmaline, kunzite and morganite, may readily be distinguished when we compare the specific gravity 3.53 for pinked topaz with

Corundum (pink sapphire)	4.03
Spinel (balas ruby)	3.60
Tourmaline (rubellite)	3.10
Spodumene (kunzite)	3.18
Beryl (morganite)	2.74

As this table indicates, the only specific gravity value among these pink gems approaching that of topaz is 3.60 for the balas ruby variety of spinel, and since spinel, as we shall presently see, is isometric in crystallization, the card test should distinguish its *single refraction* from the *double refraction* shown by a topaz gem.

SPINEL

In the days when all hard, red gems were classed as rubies, many deep red *spinels* were accorded a value as precious stones which distinctly was not theirs by right. Witness the famous "Ruby of the Black Prince," which has for centuries decorated the English Crown, and which, although considered throughout all those years as a ruby, is now known to be only a red spinel. When mineralogists separated corundum, which as we know is aluminium sesquioxide, from spinel, which is aluminate of magnesium, it was deemed advisable to consider the red spinels as a sort of inferior ruby, and so among gem merchants these spinels were known as *spinel rubies*, which in time became changed to *ruby spinels*. Also a rose-red spinel colored with chromic oxide, and resembling some of the lighter shades of corundum ruby, was designated as *balas ruby* (see color plate frontispiece).

Since ruby spinels and balas rubies, as well as all the other gem varieties of spinel, are found with the corundum gems in the gravel beds of Burma, Siam and Ceylon, it is not at all hard to understand how they should have been so long confused with these latter gem stones. Indeed it was first through a comparison of the crystals, which in the case of spinel are octahedral and resemble the diamond, that the truth became known.

In hardness spinel ranks with topaz, both gem stones being inferior to the corundum gems, but harder than other semiprecious stones. Beside the red varieties mentioned above, the Ceylon gravels furnish spinels colored orange red by iron oxide, and known as *rubicelles;* also *almandine spinels*, which are colored by manganese oxide to a violet red and a distinctive blue spinel.

In distinguishing cut stones of the spinel gems from those of other species, the principal confusion will be found with the garnet gems, since these two species alone among the colored gems are isometric and singly refracting. The card test, if carefully applied, should eliminate all the others.

As between ruby spinel, specific gravity 3.60, and pyrope garnet, specific gravity 3.78, there should be enough difference to make a gravity test distinctive. The same may be said of the difference between almandine spinel, specific gravity 3.5 to 3.7, and rhodolite garnet, specific gravity 3.84. Spinel is usually cut brilliant.

GARNET

Among all of the silicates that are recognized as accessory rock forming minerals, there are none of such common occurence and so widely distributed as the silicates of calcium, magnesium, iron, aluminium and manganese which unite in various combinations to form the *garnet* group. Garnet is found throughout the world in rocks of many types. And because of the variety of elements that compose its many species, as well as the varying conditions under which these have been found, we are prepared for a considerable array of gem stones to be comprised among the garnet gems. One feature is common to all of these garnet gems: whether red or purple, orange or green, they are linked together by the great common factor of crystal form; they are all isometric. And, moreover, the crystals that characterize them are singularly symmetrical and simple, quite unlike those of any other gem mineral.

In hardness, the garnet gems range from 6.5 to 7.5 of the Mohs scale. They vary from a little softer than quartz to a little harder than that mineral.

Just as it is an almost universal fallacy to think that all topaz gems must be yellow, so people have come to look upon all garnets as red. And, in fact, the garnet gems that are best adapted to jewelry are various shades of red, but we must not overlook the fact that other gem garnets, and some of them well known, furnish us with a wide and interesting range of color.

The reddest of all the garnet gem varieties is a magnesium aluminium silicate called *pyrope*, which is derived from a Greek word that means "fire-like." It was no doubt a pyrope garnet that gave rise to the old Talmudic legend according to which the only light in the ark of Noah was supplied by an enormous red garnet. The ruby-like quality of this color has tempted the unscrupulous to misname local occurrences of pyrope after the precious stone. In this way the pyrope garnets that accompany the diamonds in the blue ground of Kimberley have been called "Cape rubies," just as pyrope pebbles from Arizona and New Mexico, when cut, have been locally sold as "Arizona rubies."

Small deep colored pebbles of pyrope are found in considerable quantity in the neighborhood of Teplitz in Czechoslovakia and have been rose-cut into the *Bohemian garnets*, whose fine red color is the chief attraction of the peasant jewelry still sold in Prague.

An attractive light violet garnet containing oxides of iron, magnesium and aluminium comes from Macon County in North Carolina and is called *rhodolite* on account of its color. Stones cut from these gem crystals, however, are small, and the stone is little seen in the gem market.

Another red garnet is the variety containing oxides of iron and aluminium. *Almandine* or *carbuncle*, as this garnet gem is called, is deep crimson or violet red in color (see color plate frontispiece). So deep is the color of these gems that often the cabochon cutting, which is usually given to them, is modified into a rounded shell so as to present only a thin layer of the stone to the eye. The name carbuncle is derived from a Latin word signifying a little spark. These stones are mined in several parts of India, Jaipur in Rajputana being the cutting and distributing center. Large and beautiful carbuncles have also been mined in the past at Syriam in Pegu, now a part of lower Burma. A corruption of this place name has led to these stones being incorrectly called Syrian (instead of Syriam) garnets.

An orange colored garnet gem (see color plate frontispiece) from the highly productive gem gravels of Ceylon is a silicate of the oxides of calcium and aluminium, and is known by the various titles of *hessonite (essonite), cinnamon stone, hyacinth* and *jacinth*. The last two names belong properly to the yellow and orange zircon gems, which also are found in the Ceylon gravels, but it is customary for jewelers to use these terms for both gems, *and not infrequently to confuse the gems themselves*. Any doubt as to the identity of an orange yellow gem may easily be settled by the aid of a good lens, since hessonite shows a very characteristic granular appearance when the lens is focussed in the center of the stone, whereas the zircon gem will show clear double images of the bottom facets seen through the table.

A garnet gem that has a very attractive color is the aurora-red manganese aluminium garnet known as *spessartite*. Its use as a gem stone is, however, limited because clear, transparent material is difficult to find. Occasional stones have been furnished by the Ceylon localities, and some good stones have come from the Amelia Court House locality in Virginia.

The common opaque garnet that is so ubiquitous is an iron calcium silicate, known as *andradite* among mineralogists. It is, generally speaking, of no interest from the gem point of view. The exception, however, is both sensational and startling. In the latter part of the ninteenth century a number of brilliant green stones were discovered on the European side of the Ural Mountains. These were supposed at first to be emeralds, but subsequently were found to be andradite garnets of singular transparency, colored by chromic oxide. Their color ranges from olive through pistachio to a fine light emerald green. The high index of refraction, which in other garnet gems is masked by the depth of the color, renders these remarkable stones very brilliant, a quality responsible for the name *demantoid*, given them on account of their resemblance to green diamonds. Demantoids, when procurable, command the highest value per carat of any of the garnet gems.

As pointed out under spinel, garnet is one of the very few singly refracting gem stones, and should be recognized through the card test. Deep ruby colored pyrope gems might be confused with rubies, in which case resort to specific gravity determination or, better still, to a little instrument known as a dichroscope will soon settle the question of identity.

CHAPTER IX

"If heaven would make me such another world
Of one entire and perfect Crysolite."
—OTHELLO, Act V, Sc. 2.

CHAPTER IX

Semiprecious Stones
(Continued)

TOURMALINE

A very common rock forming silicate that ranks with garnet in its almost universal distribution is *tourmaline*, a complex boro silicate whose composition involves a number of the common metallic oxides. The gem varieties of this mineral are both varied and attractive in color, and since they are distinctive in this all important property of color, they surpass the garnet gems in popularity.

In hardness there is not much to choose between the tourmaline gems and those cut from garnet, both groups being about on a par with quartz, and falling below topaz and spinel. It is this relative softness that discourages the use of the tourmaline gems in ring mounts and limits their gem possibilities to such jewelry forms as pendants, brooches and beads. To these applications, however, the delicate tints of the tourmaline gem stones bring a peculiar charm, a fact long recognized by the Chinese lapidaries, whose pendants carved from pink and light yellowish green tourmaline are only beginning to be appreciated by our Western culture.

[113]

Although tourmaline is distributed with cosmopolitan impartiality all over the world in such rocks as pegmatitic granite schists and limestones, crystals of gem quality are to be found in certain places where they are generally speaking associated with some of the other gem minerals. For instance, the State of Minas Geraes in Brazil, which is a very productive source of gem topaz, also yields deeply colored tourmaline in blue, green and reddish pink. The deep blue color, described as an indigo blue, has led to the naming of the blue tourmaline *indicolite*. Bottle green stones with a trace of blue in their color tone are known as *Brazilian emeralds*, although their color is far from being an emerald green (see color plate frontispiece).

Rubellite, the pink gem variety, also occurs at the Brazilian localities both in solidly colored crystals and in curiously parti-colored prisms, of which the core is pink, edged with white, and the outer rim is green.

A reversal of the colors of the Brazilian rimmed crystals is to be seen in the parti-colored tourmaline from Pala, Ramola, and Misa Grande in California, the crystals from these localities often displaying a green core edged with white and surrounded by a rim of pink rubellite. From the California localities also come the magnificent rose red (see color plate frontispiece) and pink rubellite, as well as fine light green gem crystals.

Elsewhere in the United States gem tourmaline, notably in the lighter shades, has been found at Paris, Hebron and Auburn in Maine, and at Haddam Neck in Connecticut. Although the deeper colors, so characteristic of Brazil, are by no means lacking among the New England tourmalines, the delicate lilac, light smoky green and greenish yellow are notable among the charming gamut of colors displayed by these stones, and here it would be well to point out that no gem mineral, with the possible exception of the Ceylon corundum gems, presents so many variously colored stones from one locality as does tourmaline. To such an extent is this true that it is almost impossible definitely to place a tourmaline gem of a certain color as coming from a given place.

The Russian localities on both sides of the Ural Mountains, which, as we have seen, furnished splendid topaz and aquamarine gems, have also been famous for wonderfully colored tourmalines. Mursinka and other places in the neighborhood of Ekaterinburg and Nertschinsk in the Province of Transbaikal have produced tourmaline of various shades of blue, green and pink.

The island of Madagascar has produced tourmaline gems in several unique colors, among which a reddish brown is perhaps the one that best lends itself to a description. But as with many of the other colors of this variegated gem, words give only a dim picture of their subtle attractiveness, and the gems should be seen rather than visualized from a description.

The Island of Elba is famed for its light colored pink, yellowish and green stones. These are often parti-colored, the two extremities of the slender prismatic crystals exhibiting different colors. There is a very significant connection between this uneven distribution of color in tourmaline and the crystal form and physical properties of this mineral. The prismatic crystals of tourmaline, which have for their cross section a triangle with rounded sides, are differently modified at their two extremities, giving an aspect of polar symmetry to the two ends of these crystals. Electric and other physical properties emphasize this polarity, which, no doubt, is explainable by assuming that the atomic structure of tourmaline is also polar, and the disposition of the coloring matter is doubtless traceable to the same cause.

Tourmaline is dichroic to a very considerable degree. A cube cut from the center of a crystal of even color will appear much darker when viewed in the direction of the length of the prism than when viewed *across* this direction. Lapidaries make use of this property in cutting deep colored stones with the table parallel to the axis of the crystal, so as to lighten the color, or the reverse for a very light colored stone.

No difficulty should be encountered in the determination of a stone cut from tourmaline. In addition to the fact that the specific gravity 3.0 to 3.2 does not approximate that of any mineral with which it might be confused, the very marked dichroism of these gems renders a test with the dichroscope very positive and distinctive.

Tourmaline gems are usually given a combination cut, a brilliant cut crown with a stepped cut pavilion.

ZIRCON

As an accessory mineral in such crystalline rocks as granites and gneisses, the silicate of zirconium known as *zircon* is far less common than either tourmaline or garnet. We are therefore prepared to find the zircon gems not only more restricted in distribution but less well known than the rank and file of the semi-precious stones previously described. Zircon is essentially an Oriental gem. It is much oftener met with in the bazaars of Ceylon and Burma than in the jewelry shops of Fifth Avenue and the Rue de la Paix. Its very name is said to come from the Arabic, *zarqun*, vermilion, or the Persian, *zargun*, gold colored. The sixth of the seven Moslem heavens is said to be composed of *yellow jacinth*, which is one of the names for gem zircon.

The chief source of the zircon gems is Ceylon, where they are found in the gem gravel, together with corundum gems, spinels and hessonite garnets.

In hardness zircon ranks at 7.5 of the Mohs scale, rather harder than quartz, but not so hard as topaz. It is therefore not altogether suitable as a ring stone, but as if in compensation for this short-coming, Nature has endowed the zircon gems with a range of color that is highly attractive and an index of refraction that enables them, when cut, to rival the diamond in brilliance and fire.

A variety the color of which has been described as aurora red is known as *hyacinth* or *jacinth*. Perhaps a closer approximation to this color would be to compare it to the juice of ripe plums. Nor is the name hyacinth altogether a good one, although by jewelers it has been applied to all of the zircon gems. The diffi-culty is that it has been applied as well to hessonite garnet, and that neither stone resembles the well known flower in color. Hyacinth zircons in small stones have been found at Expailly, in Auvergne, as well as in the famous Ceylon gravels, thus furnish-ing France with its single gem stone. Mudgee, New South Wales, also produces red zircons of a considerable depth of color.

In the magnificent golden yellow, honey yellow, greenish brown and leaf green gems, however, Ceylon has no rival (see color plate frontispiece), and it is indeed difficult to see why these stones, which enjoyed a brief popularity in the late nineteenth century, ever ceased to be desirable. Generally speaking, the vari-ous yellow shades and especially the white zircons produced by heat from stones of these colors are called *jargoons*. When cut, these latter have the distinction of more perfectly imitating dia-monds than any other white stones.

With all the striking and attractive colors characteristic of the zircon gems, it seems indeed strange that the only variety of this gem mineral that is at present at all popular should be of an arti-ficially produced color. This is a steely blue zircon gem of great brilliancy and dispersion when cut. The color is said to be obtained by heating the yellow Siamese stones. Although actual blue gem crystals have long been known, these modern "blued" zircons far surpass them in both color and fire.

The ease with which the zircon gems may be determined rests on the very marked double refraction characteristic of this mineral. Even with stones as small as one carat, a good hand lens will clearly show two images of the edges between the back facets as seen through the table.

Zircons are usually cut as brilliants or are given a combination brilliant step cut. The former is better adapted to blue zircons and other light colored stones, and the latter to hyacinths and deep honey yellow stones.

PERIDOT

Somewhat better known than zircon, but far from achieving the popularity that it deserves, is the gem variety of chrysolite known as *peridot,* a silicate of magnesium and iron. Among the bewilderingly various colors displayed by others among the gem stones, peridot stands apart as characterized by one constant and unmistakable color, a fine rich olive green. So pronounced is this olive color that peridot has often been called the evening emerald.

It is a relatively soft gem stone, falling a little below quartz in hardness; and for this reason its use in ring mounts is not to be encouraged. There are few gems, however, that lend themselves to the many adaptations of modern jewelry with such marked success, and the growing demand for peridots threatens to exceed the rather meager supply.

The mineral chrysolite, of which peridot is a gem variety, is a characteristic accessory mineral in igneous rocks, notably in those of a basaltic character, and since this rather tends to limit the possibilities of its occurrence, peridot has been found in relatively few places. The principal source of gem crystals is the Island of Zebirget, or St. John, in the western part of the Red Sea, about opposite the Egyptian port of Berenice. This locality has long been famous for peridots of deep color, such stones being usually called *Levantine peridots* (see color plate frontispiece). Of an even deeper shade, with somewhat less yellow in its tone, are the peridots from Burma. Few of these, however, come to Western markets.

Small pebbles of peridot are to be found in considerable quantity in parts of Arizona and New Mexico, associated with the pyrope garnets mentioned in the last chapter, and locally known of *Job's tears*. Since these are light in color and incapable of furnishing any but small stones, they can not compete with the magnificent Levantine stones, which latter often cut to gems of 30 or 40 carats in weight.

Light green stones of pleasing shade are also found in Queensland. As with the zircon gems, the best means of determining peridots is furnished by their strong double refraction. In stones of ten carats or more the unaided eye is capable of detecting the apparent double images of the back facets as seen through the table. This simple test, coupled with their characteristic color, renders the recognition of peridots a very easy matter.

The forms of cutting usually adopted for peridots are the step cut or a combination brilliant step cut, depending somewhat on the shape of the girdle and the size of the stone.

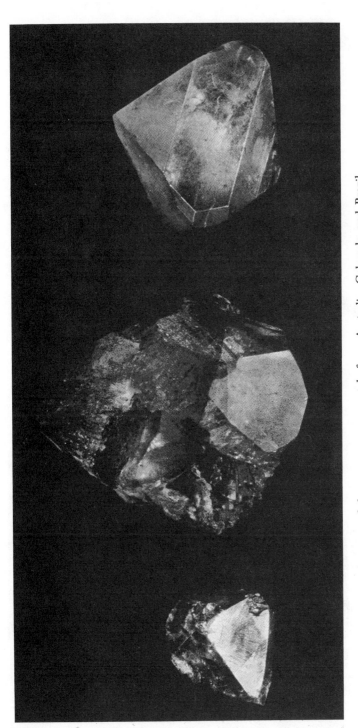

A group of three topaz gem crystals from Australia, Colorado and Brazil, showing the typical symmetry of topaz crystals.

Courtesy of American Museum of Natural History

A gem crystal of garnet (Spessar-tite) from Raymond, Maine. Note the high degree of symmetry in this crystal, which is typical of garnet.
Courtesy of American Museum of Natural History

Bohemian garnets set in typical Bohemian peasant jewelry.

The Vatican Cameo. Head of Christ carved in essonite garnet.
Courtesy of American Museum of Natural History

With its 444 perfectly propor-tioned facets this blue Topaz is a marvelous expression of the art of the lapidary.
Courtesy of American Museum of Natural History

A group of gem crystals of tourmaline (rubellite) with quartz from Pala, San Diego County, California. These magnificent crystals are highly typical of the triangular tourmaline prism.

Courtesy of American Museum of Natural History

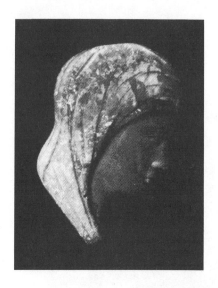

Cameo head carved from opal matrix
from Stuart Range, South Australia.
Courtesy of American Museum of Natural History

A brilliant cut stone. Zircon.
*Courtesy of American Museum
of Natural History*

Cameo head carved from opal matrix
from Mayneside, West Queensland.
Courtesy of American Museum of Natural History

CHAPTER X

*"But he took us through his palace and, my lads,
   as I'm a sinner,
We walked into an opal like a sunset colored cloud."*
                                    —ALFRED NOYES

CHAPTER X

Chrysoberyl and Opal

I<small>T</small> would seem that in interpolating, as it were, an extra class of gem values between precious and semiprecious stones, we were drawing a fine distinction and creating complications in a matter that should be essentially a simple one. In point of fact, the two gem minerals now to be described may be said to have advanced from the semiprecious rating of the last century and are, on a basis of present day values, now within the margin of value covered by grades of acknowledged precious stones which are, however, not of the ranking quality.

CHRYSOBERYL

The aluminate of beryllium that is known among mineralogists as *chrysoberyl* is recognized among dealers in gems mainly through two rather rare special varieties, *Oriental cat's eye* and *alexandrite*. It is harder than any of the gem stones except diamond and corundum, and is therefore adaptable to all forms of jewelry settings, including ring mounts.

Of the several gem varieties furnished by chrysoberyl, the least well known and at the same time the most attractive is the yellow gem incorrectly called chrysolite by jewelers (see color plate frontispiece). It would seem that a more proper designation for this variety would be *yellow chrysoberyl*, since the term chrysolite is recognized among mineralogists as designating the magnesium silicate which furnishes the gem stone peridot.

Yellow chrysoberyl probably owes its color, which is a pale yellowish green much resembling that of the liqueur Chartreuse, to a small amount of ferrous oxide. Beautiful gem crystals of complex orthorhombic symmetry come from Minas Novas, in the State of Minas Geraes, Brazil. These, although lucidly transparent to the eye, occasionally contain hollow inclusions which produce in a cabochon cut stone the semblance of a floating ray of light. Splendid yellow chrysoberyl is also to be found in Ceylon in yellowish brown, honey yellow and olive green colors, as well as in the typical chartreuse yellow tint.

The presence of hollow tube-like inclusions in parallel position within the gem crystals of certain kinds of chrysoberyls is responsible for a peculiar and very beautiful effect of chatoyancy developed in cabochon cut stones. These *cymophanes* or Oriental cat's eyes are never perfectly clear, but exhibit *through* their translucency a band of reflected light which moves with the position of the eye, and, in some instances, includes the entire half of the stone in the effect (see color plate frontispiece). The moving beam of light in a chrysoberyl cat's eye is comparable in cause and in effect to the star exhibited by a star sapphire or a star ruby. In the former case the hollow inclusions are distributed within the stone in one direction only; in the latter they are distributed in three directions parallel to the six-sided cross section of the crystal.

Oriental cat's eyes, as their name implies, are mostly derived from Ceylon. In color they range from a greenish yellow, merging into the transparent effect noted as occurring in the Brazilian stones, to a fine olive green, which is the more desirable tint.

A commoner and less valuable kind of cat's eye is composed of quartz enclosing asbestos-like fibers in parallel position. This stone, although giving a reflected band of light, is rendered opaque by reason of the included fibers and entirely lacks the opalescent gleam characteristic of the Oriental cat's eye. Both kinds are cut with rather a high cabochon cutting, oval in girdle, the long axis lying across the parallel inclusions, which is also the direction of the line of reflected light.

In the year 1830, on an anniversary of the birth of the then reigning Czar, Alexander II, a beautiful and remarkable gem variety of chrysoberyl was discovered in the emerald mines near Ekaterinburg, Russia. As a consequence of this coincidence this gem was named *alexandrite,* and for nearly a hundred years was the acknowledged national gem of Russia.

Alexandrite is always found in twinned crystals that appear to be hexagonal, although actually orthorhombic. The color of the Russian stones, which were obtained from Takowaja, as well as Ekaterinburg, changes with the quality of the light that they reflect. In daylight they appear a somewhat muddy bluish green, but when illuminated by artificial light of yellow quality, this color changes to a deep raspberry-red. This odd change of color is due the delicate balance maintained in the absorption color, a change in the color of the light transmitted being sufficient to produce a marked change in the color of the stone.

Alexandrites are now obtained mainly from Ceylon. The Oriental stones, although a little lighter in color, more transparent and with less contrast in the absorption colors, run to considerably larger sizes. Ceylon alexandrites are olive or bottle green by daylight, and a lighter and less vivid red by artificial light. The color in alexandrite is said to be due to chromic oxide. In varieties other than cat's eye, chrysoberyl gems are usually cut as brilliants.

OPAL

"Who can look into an opal without seeing a rainbow?" Here, at last, is one gem stone that has no distinctive color, because it combines in itself all of the colors. *Opal* is one of the very few minerals that do not crystallize. It is a solidified jelly composed of silica with a small and somewhat variable proportion of water. In the precious varieties of opal, those which furnish the opal gem stones, this amorphous jelly-like mass in the process of hardening was traversed by a multitude of small cracks. It is the presence of these cracks, which were subsequently filled with a later deposit of opal, that gives to this remarkable gem its singular play of color. The light that is returned to the eye, after being reflected from the surfaces of these exceedingly fine cracks, is subjected to interference and broken up into colors just as light reflected from any film, such as a soap-bubble, is broken up by interfering waves of light. The thinner and more uniform the series of cracks, the finer and broader the flash of reflected color.

The oldest opal mines are located near Kaschau in Hungary, or what is now Czechoslovakia, and in all probability they furnished examples of this marvelous stone to the Romans. Pliny described them in glowing terms, likening their colors to the "burning fire of the carbuncle, the glorious purple of the amethyst, the sea green of the emerald."

Hungarian opals, with their delicate play of color, very much split up and patchy, ruled supreme up to the late years of the nineteenth century, and were sometimes referred to as *Oriental opals*, because they were carried to the Orient and then shipped to Europe. More frequently they were called *harlequin opals*, on account of the patches of color characterizing them.

The opals of Mexico, that during the nineteenth century shared with those of Hungary what popular favor was left to these stones by the superstition of ill luck, came mostly from Quere-taro in the state of the same name. They are notably of the fire opal variety with a reddish ground color or with the angry smouldering red glows shooting up through milky layers of trans-lucent ground mass (see color plate frontispiece). A few small and inferior opals have also been found in Honduras.

Today the supremacy in the production of fine opals has come to the newest of the continents, Australia. As so often happens in such matters, the first of the Australian opal fields was accidentally discovered, by a kangaroo hunter, who picked up an attractive piece of opal in the neighborhood of White Cliffs in New South Wales.

The White Cliffs opals are not unlike those from Hungary, but they show broader flashes of color and they are found in masses capable of furnishing larger stones. At this place also the hot siliceous solutions have been instrumental in the replacement of certain organic remains by opal. In this way it is not at all unusual to find fossil shells and bones of extinct animals and even wood entirely replaced by gem opal.

The more important Australian opal fields, however, are those which were later discovered along the boundary between New South Wales and Queensland. Unlike the White Cliff stones, or indeed any opals previously known, these stones are notably dark in color by transmitted light and occur in a jasper and an iron colored sandstone matrix, producing an effect that thoroughly justifies the term *black opals* which has been given to them. Black opals come from Lightning Ridge, New South Wales, and Barcoo River in Queensland, and for depth and brilliancy of color rank supreme among opals (see color plate frontispiece). None who has not seen them can imagine the quality of these opalescent colors, which against the black background of the body of the stone flash scintillating blazes of red, orange, blue, green and purple.

Quite recently a deposit of light colored opal has been found in the Stuart Range of South Australia. In the opals from this field the range of color is lighter, more ethereal than that which characterizes even the Hungarian stones. The prevailing shades contain more greenish yellow, light orange and flame colors, and seem to lack the blues and purples. The matrix of these Stuart Range stones is also characteristic, being a volcanic rock of a light grayish flesh color, against which the faint colors of the opal give a charming effect.

The very character of the structure of the opal gems has in it the elements of disaster. As one would expect, any stone so riddled with incipient breaks is very liable to permanent fracture, and slight but sudden changes of temperature are often enough to reduce a beautiful and valuable gem to a mere heap of shattered fragments. Perhaps this is the real reason for the tradition of ill luck that has been ascribed to this beautiful gem stone. And why not? Surely the loss of a prized possession is enough of a misfortune to justify the legend. With reasonable care, however, an opal should have a long and vivid life, reflecting in its many colors all the moods of its wearer.

CHAPTER XI

"As for rock crystal, it was the universal opinion of ancient naturalists, and the belief, indeed almost to our own time, that it was water congealed to that hardness, by long continued and intense cold."

—ANCIENT MINERALOGY
BY N. F. MOORE (1834)

CHAPTER XI

The Quartz Gems

THERE is probably no single substance on earth that is so obvious from the point of view of the student of minerals as quartz. It is to be found in all sorts of places, and in all kinds of rocks, from the grain of sand on the beach to the rock formation on the mountain side. Because quartz is so universally present under varying conditions, it is not at all strange that we should find it in an almost endless variety of phases. To be sure, as gem stones, these varieties of quartz are not, generally speaking, valuable. They constitute the stones that are priced by the pennyweight rather than by the carat. For this very reason, however, they hold a unique place in the scale of gem values as materials out of which we may fashion such jewelry as beads, as well as the host of small art objects that are usually decorated with engraving and carving.

Chemically, quartz consists of the combination of the two commonest elements in the earth's crust, oxygen and silicon. When pure, quartz is without color, clear and limpid as water. The various colors—purple, yellow, brown, pink, etc.— that lend variety to this universal mineral are probably due to small amounts of metallic oxides, making the gamut of color analogous in origin to that of the corundum gems rather than like the colors of garnets and tourmalines, which owe their various tints to actual differences in composition.

In considering the very many kinds of quartz, we must also recognize the fact that there are varieties which form in definite crystals of the well known six-sided, prismatic shape, and other varieties which, like opal, are never found in crystals, but always in rounded masses, formed of layers. We might compare the quartz varieties of the first kind to the six-sided snow crystals, and those of the second phase to the rounded icicles of freezing water. In the one instance the substance of the mineral (because water is just as much a mineral as is quartz) has been assembled in a regular fashion to form a crystal, and in the other this regularity is, to the eye at least, entirely lacking.

It is among the *crystallized* quartz varieties that we find in general the materials from which facetted gem stones are cut; and among the imperfectly crystallized or *gel* varieties that we look for the materials for carved objects. This distinction, however, is far from being a binding one, especially in relation to the carved objects fashioned by the Chinese from any of the quartz varieties that please the eye and that lend themselves to expressing the art of these clever and highly skilled lapidaries.

ROCK CRYSTAL

Crystallized quartz absolutely free from any coloring matter is known as *rock crystal*. In the time of Pliny such limpid, water clear silica was supposed to be simply petrified water, a belief that was only abandoned when the spread of knowledge in the eighteenth century caused this, as well as many other mineralogical myths, to be decried.

In relation to present day jewelry uses, rock crystal may be said to supply material for necklace beads, either as facetted beads or as the small flat separators used between beads of other materials which are known as *rondels*.

Rock crystal is preeminently a medium in which carved art objects are wrought. Since the supply of material for these is limited only by the size of flawless quartz crystals obtainable, it is obvious that the value of such pieces depends on their size, and especially on the amount and quality of work involved in the fashioning of them.

To the layman the best known of these rock crystal carvings are the highly polished spheres produced in all sizes up to a foot in diameter by the Japanese lapidaries. Such rock crystal balls are now, no doubt, being made by methods involving some variation of the turning lathe introduced into Japan from Europe or America. As recently, however, as the closing decade of the last century, the methods and tools employed in their cutting were of the most primitive sort. The writer is familiar with a set of small rock crystal balls in all stages of completion, which, together with the simple tools employed in their manufacture, were brought back from Japan in the "nineties" by the late Dr. Thomas Egleston. The tools consisted of a long, narrow piece of steel, shaped somewhat like a carpenter's gauge, and a joint of the male bamboo, both of these being of a size commensurate with the diameter of the ball to be cut. A quartz fragment of appropriate rough shape was rubbed against the concave steel edge until the rough corners were chipped and worn off, and the piece assumed a rough spherical shape. The smaller irregularities were then reduced by rubbing with the bamboo joints, into the pores of which quartz dust had worked its way and so acted as an abrasive. Polishing was done with a fresh piece of bamboo, either charged with rouge or uncharged with any abrasive. Months of arduous labor must have gone to the making of one of these rock crystal spheres as fashioned in this way; and since a flawless rock crystal of greater diameter through the prism than the diameter of the resulting ball is required, it follows that the value of them increases very rapidly with an increase in diameter. A rock crystal ball four inches in diameter is worth a great deal more than twice the value of one of two inches in diameter, and probably nearer in the neighborhood of four times this value.

Two very simple tests suffice to detect a glass imitation of a rock crystal ball. In the first place, glass is seldom free from round bubbles, which even when very small are visible with the aid of a hand lens. Also, quartz, although doubly refracting to only a relatively small extent, will still show double images of fine lines viewed through even as small a thickness as an inch and a half. The double refraction test is easily applied by shifting the ball in question over a sheet of printed matter so that periods or dotted i's will be seen through different directions. If the material is rock crystal, a position will be found in which *two images* of the printed type will show *through* the ball.

In addition to the Japanese rock crystal spheres, clear quartz has been used in China for several centuries as a material for the carving of a great many beautiful and interesting small objects, such as vases, snuff bottles, figurines, ink boxes, incense burners and pendants.

With the exception of the covered boxes of square or polygonal shape, designed to hold india ink, all of the above mentioned objects have also been made from amethyst and rose quartz, and sometimes also from smoky quartz. Frequently an area of amethyst inclosed in a mass of rock crystal is adapted in the carving to represent some feature of the design with great taste and skill.

In sharp contrast to the freedom and native grace that mark the Chinese carvings in rock crystal are the laboriously elaborate carved objects in this medium that were produced in the Imperial Lapidary Works at Ekaterinburg, Russia, during the nineteenth century. These include such Victorian ornaments as formal "coupes," seals, paper weights, flat dishes, as well as occasional figurines, cane and umbrella handles and such trifles. These were all executed with an elaborate formality that gave to them an almost architectural aspect in keeping with the period that produced them. Their very elaborateness, however, was emphasized by a rare skill in execution and a considerable taste in the combining of matte and polished surfaces in the working out of the designs.

AMETHYST

The purple variety of quartz known as *amethyst* has been employed as a gem stone since very early times, and the appreciation of this gem material has extended down through the ages, reaching its culmination in the last century, when facetted amethyst gems were justly popular. A recent swing of the pendulum of fashion seems to be reviving this beautiful purple gem stone. Although amethyst colored quartz is of very common occurrence in rocks of almost every country, the deepest colored and most sought after gem material is somewhat limited to certain well defined deposits. Russian gem amethysts, often called *Siberian amethysts*, are mined in several places in the Ural Mountains, notably at Mursinka, near Ekaterinburg (see color plate frontispiece). These stones are very deep in color, the rich purple tone being mixed with some red, a combined color which is readily recognized by one experienced in handling amethysts. Brazilian amethysts from the state of Rio Grande do Sul are also deep purple in color, as are also those from Uruguay. Fine stones have been taken from the gem gravels of Ceylon, from Madagascar and from various parts of the United States.

The disposal of the color throughout crystals of amethyst quartz is not always evenly regular, many gem fragments showing a patchy coloring, which detracts materially from the beauty of the cut gem. In a number of instances this unevenness of color follows the twinning of the quartz crystals, giving alternate triangular sectors of purple and white quartz, best visible in sections at right angles to the prism edges.

Amethyst has from traditional times been the stone used in ecclesiastical rings as worn by bishops and other church prelates. It is usually cut in some variation of the combination step brilliant cutting.

CITRINE

A light yellow variety of quartz, which probably owes its color to a trace of ferric iron, was much used in the Victorian period of the last century, and was erroneously called "topaz." The more proper designation for this stone is *citrine* (see color plate frontispiece), but the term "topaz" has been so long in use among jewelers in connection with it that the true topaz has now come to be denoted by the name *precious topaz*.

In color citrine is smoky and dead, lacking the lively orange lights that characterize precious topaz, as well as the brilliancy and fire so apparent in the Oriental topaz variety of the corundum gems. It has now entirely retired from popularity and is to be found only in examples of Victorian jewelry.

CAIRNGORM

The smoky variety of crystallized quartz, colored various shades of grayish brown by organic matter, has long been a favorite gem stone among the Scotch, and is termed *cairngorm* or *cairngorm stone* because large crystals of deep and even color are found at Cairngorm, Banffshire, Scotland.

Cairngorm has a tendency to pass by insensible gradations of color into citrine, both stones sometimes being termed *Scotch topaz*. Very deep smoky quartz often goes by the name of *morion*.

A deep colored smoky quartz from the Province of Cordova, Spain, assumes a yellow color on being heated and is known as *Spanish topaz*. The quality of this artificial color is so much nearer that of precious topaz that the specific gravity should be taken in questionable cases to distinguish true topaz, with a gravity of 3.53, from Spanish topaz, whose gravity is that of quartz, i.e., 2.66.

ROSE QUARTZ

The pink or rose red quartz, which may owe its color to titanium, belongs among the gem stones derived from crystallized quartz, although it is very seldom found in actual crystals. The color is ordinarily more or less translucent, the clearer varieties often having a close resemblance to light colored rubellite. A little experience in judging these colors, however, is sufficient to enable one to differentiate the two stones.

Rose quartz is now employed in the fashioning of necklace beads and of the many smaller articles carved by the Chinese.

MILKY QUARTZ

Closely allied to rose quartz in translucency as well as in jewelry uses is the milky white quartz variety known as *milky quartz*.

A group of carvings in rock crystal showing the ornate and formal treatment characteristic of the Russian lapidary artists of the last century.

Courtesy of American Museum of Natural History

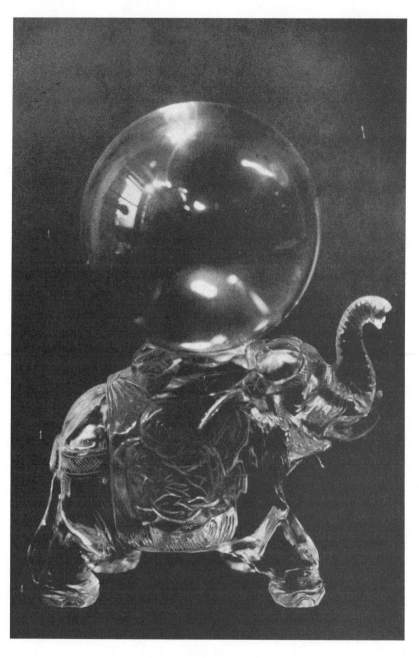

A perfect ball carved from flawless rock crystal by a Japanese craftsman, who also carved the realistic rock crystal elephant upon which it rests.

Courtesy of American Museum of Natural History

A covered vase carved from rock crystal showing the grace of outline combined with high manual skill achieved by the Chinese school of carving.

Courtesy of American Museum of Natural History

A seal carved from rock crystal showing Atlas supporting the world. This is executed with great detail and skill by a Russian lapidary of the last century.

CHAPTER XII

*"Lo in yon brilliant window niche
How statue-like I see thee stand,
The agate lamp within thy hand."*
—To Helen
by Edgar Allan Poe

CHAPTER XII

The Quartz Gems
(*Continued*)

QUARTZ, whether formed as part of an igneous rock or from a silica bearing solution in a vein, is usually the last mineral to be deposited. This is why we often find more or less perfectly formed minerals enclosed in quartz, the former representing an early stage of mineral depositions, while the latter exhibits a later period of mineral formation.

Much the same sequence is indicated when we find weeds and rushes enclosed in the ice of a frozen pond.

The gem stones furnished by the various included minerals contained in quartz constitute a division of the large family of quartz gems that belongs rather to the phase of the crystallized quartz varieties than to the gel phases to be presently discussed.

RUTILATED QUARTZ

Rock crystal containing long, fine, needle-like crystals of rutile is often called *sagenite*, because the reddish-brown interlacing needles resemble a net (Latin, *sagena*). Many fanciful names have also been given to this stone, such as *flêches d'amour* (arrows of love) and *Venus's hairstone*.

Quite similar in effect is the clear quartz including long thin crystals of tourmaline, of hornblends and of actinolite (called also *Thetis hairstone*).

Occasionally the mineral included in quartz is present in closely packed parallel fibers of an asbestiform texture. Such stones when cut cabochon display a chatoyant effect, the line of reflected light lying across the direction of the included fibers. These are known as *quartz cat's eye*, or ordinary *cat's eye* as distinct from Oriental cat's eye described under chrysoberyl.

Quartz cat's eyes of fine quality come from India and Ceylon. Bavarian stones of this variety are found in the Fichtelgebirge and are often erroneously called *Hungarian cat's eyes*.

TIGER EYE

A variety of amphibole asbestos which is known as *crocidolite* occurs in the neighborhood of Griquatown, Griqualand, West South Africa, where the silk-like fibers of this mineral have been impregnated with quartz. Originally this stone was colored a grayish blue. During the infiltration of the silica, however, the iron oxide which was the cause of the blueish color was further oxidized to a rich ocherous brown or even to a mahogany red. The yellow brown stone has been called *tiger eye*, and the grayish blue phase, *hawk eye*. Both are highly chatoyant, and often the two colors are mingled in very pleasing effects. Small ornaments have been carved from tiger eye.

PRASE

Quartz enclosing hair-like actinolite fibers arranged at haphazard constitutes the dark leek-green stone known as prase, also called *mother of emerald* because at one time it was erroneously supposed to be the matrix or mother-rock of emerald. Prase of the deepest and best color comes from the Erzgebirge in Saxony.

AVENTURINE

An ornamental variety of quartz which encloses minute flakes of hematite or mica is called *aventurine*, and should not be confused with the feldspar gem stone of the same name, to be described in a subsequent chapter. The small scales enclosed within this stone reflect back the light in a highly pleasing manner. A green aventurine enclosing fine plates of chrome mica is found in the Bellary District of Madras, India, and is very popular as a decorative stone for the carving of bowls, trays and other small objects.

Siberian aventurine owes its very attractive light orange color and lively glitter to included reddish mica. It occurs at Kossulina in the Ural Mountains.

It is among the multitudinous varieties of imperfectly crystallized quartz that we encounter an almost bewildering number of gem stones and gem stone names. To such an extent is this true that in this chapter many of the more obscure gem synonyms have been omitted through lack of space and for the sake of clarity.

CHALCEDONY

Just as rock crystal gave us a starting point in the enumeration of the varieties of crystallized quartz, so the relatively colorless gel variety of silica known as *chalcedony* constitutes a point of departure in the discussion of quartz gem stones of this phase.

Chalcedony is translucent rather than transparent and is usually faintly colored a milky white, gray, blueish or yellowish. It is found in stalactitic masses with rounded, concentric surfaces. The blueish gray chalcedony is sometimes called *sapphirine*, a term the use of which is not to be encouraged, since it is close in etymology to the blue corundum gem, as well as being identical with a rare non-gem mineral.

Chalcedony was much used by the ancients as a medium for engraved gems; examples are to be found among the cylinders of Assyria and Babylon, the intagli of Greece and the oval talismanic seals of Persia. Its modern gem uses include necklace beads, bowls and small ornamental objects carved mostly in Western Germany. To these we must add the figurines and vases carved from chalcedony by the Chinese.

Of even greater importance from the viewpoint of the antique use of gems is the translucent red chalcedony known as *carnelian*.

The lively orange-red color of this gem stone, combined with the uniformity of its texture, has rendered it preeminently the stone adaptable to seals and intagli. It has long been used in this way by gem engravers of all ages and countries, and occupies a prominent place among the materials employed for very primitive necklace beads. These uses have endured to the present day, as is evidenced by the popularity of carnelian as a material for necklace beads, and especially for the beautifully carved pendants fashioned by Chinese lapidaries. Otherwise the uses of carnelian are much the same as stated for chalcedony.

SARD

A variant of carnelian, sometimes recognized as a distinct gem stone of the quartz family, is the brown to yellow *sard*. Although sard shares with carnelian the prestige of antiquity of use, there seems to be little doubt that the "Sardus stone" of the Bible refers to the latter rather than to the former gem stone. Both carnelian and sard owe their color to iron oxide.

CHRYSOPRASE

Perhaps the most attractive of the colored phases of chalcedony is the apple green *chrysoprase*, which owes its color to nickel oxide. This was at one time in considerable demand as a decorative stone, and its many uses included slabs for interior decoration. The chief sources, the mines at Rosemitz in Silesia, have not produced any chrysoprase for over a hundred years, and in spite of its beautiful color this stone is now very little known.

All of the chalcedony and agate varieties of quartz are somewhat porous, a fact that is advantageously used in the artificial coloring of these varieties. Particularly is this method of artificial coloring used to imitate chrysoprase by treating grayish chalcedony with a solution of nickel oxide. The *Swiss lapis* that was quite popular in the last century for lockets, watch chain charms and such small objects was colored a Prussian blue by soaking cracked quartz in a solution of potassium ferrocyanide.

AGATE

The gel phase of silica deposition formed by successive layers of quartz produces, as we have seen, the variously colored varieties of chalcedony. When we consider that the constitution and consequently the color of the quartz forming solutions may undergo a change or many changes in the process, we come to an understanding of the significance of the many and variously colored layers that constitute the quartz variety known as *agate*.

Because of the stalactitic character of all of the gel phases of quartz, the successive colored bands or layers of agate are frequently rounded and nodular as to surface, and ring-like when these surfaces are cut across in the process of making flat slabs of agate or in the carving of ornamental objects. The banding, however, is apt to follow very irregular surfaces, due to the merging of several rounded groups of layers, which roughly conform to the irregularities of the cavity or other surfaces on which the silica was deposited. Especially fine agates come from Southern Brazil and Uruguay.

ONYX; SARDONYX

The colors of the superposed layers of agate have been utilized by lapidaries skilled in the cutting of cameos to give shading and contrast to their work. A favorite contrast in color among such cameos is furnished by a white layer superposed upon a black one, the combination taking the name *onyx* from the deep black background color. Where a white layer contrasted with one of carnelian or sard is used, the combination is known as *sardonyx*.

The term *nicolo* is sometimes given to an onyx in which the light colored layer in which the design of the cameo is to be cut is translucent blueish white.

MOSS AGATE

The gel quartz varieties sometimes include other previously formed minerals. When these are present, they ordinarily take the form of incipient crystallizations rather than perfectly formed crystals, giving rise to the various forms of *moss agate*, which, contrary to a popular fallacy, contains no moss, fossilized or otherwise.

The brown or black moss-like patterns characteristic of the *Mocha stones* of India and of the moss agates of our own Western States are produced by manganese oxide, which during the time when the chalcedony was being consolidated from a silica jelly, formed a multitude of branching crystalline patterns, similar to, and produced in the same way as, window frost.

A form of moss agate which is used to a certain extent for carved objects in China shows dendritic or tree-like inclusions of greenish chlorite enclosed in chalcedony. The effect of this

Chinese variation of chalcedony-enclosed mineral is like sea weed rather than moss, particularly as the green is often interspersed with red and ocher colored inclusions.

JASPER

Iron oxide, which for the most part gives color to the various kinds of chalcedony, when present in still greater amounts in the gel phases of quartz, produces opaque, deeply colored varieties of this kaleidoscopic mineral. These deep colored, opaque quartz varieties are included under the general term of *jasper*.

The most familiar of the jasper colors is a deep red, varying in shade from a vermilion to a dull Indian red. Egyptian jasper, which, as its name indicates, was originally found near Cairo, is ocher-yellow deepening to chestnut brown and is often banded in attractively colored red-yellow or red-green stripes.

Jasper was a favorite material with the Russian lapidaries of the nineteenth century, who employed the red, green, slate gray, yellow and various combinations of these colors in Siberian jasper for the multitude of small carved objects which they produced.

Bloodstone, or *heliotrope*, consists of jasper of which the body color is a dark green mottled with irregular spots of blood red. The best bloodstone comes from India and from the Ural Mountains.

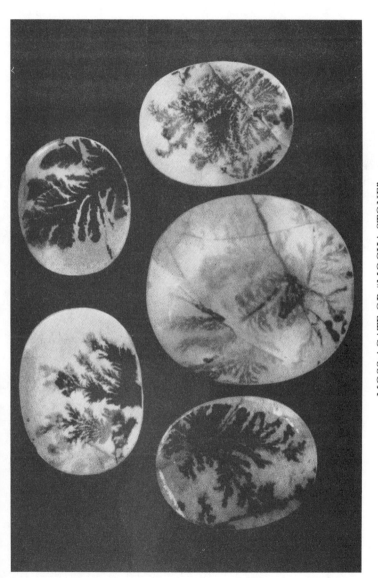

MOSS AGATE OR "MOCHA STONE"
Courtesy of American Museum of Natural History

A thin carved bowl made from stalactitic chalcedony. Note the circular patterns
formed by very close concentric rings, giving the effect of rotary motion.

Courtesy of American Museum of Natural History

"PAS DE DANSE"

A figurine carved from blueish chalcedony by G. Tonnelier of Paris. This statuette was owned by Mr. Morgan, who gave it to Mr. Charles Lanier, by whose gift it is now in the Morgan Gem Collection.

Courtesy of American Museum of Natural History

A compote or flat vase carved from gray Russian jasper by Kalugin in 1871, at the Russian Imperial Lapidary Works.
Courtesy of American Museum of Natural History

A figure of K'wan Yin, the Chinese "Goddess of Mercy" carved from yellow jasper (moss jasper) by a Chinese artisan of the Ming period.
Courtesy of American Museum of Natural History

CHAPTER XIII

"... he made
An image of his God in gold and pearl
With turquoise diadem and human eyes."
—EVARRA AND HIS GODS (KIPLING)

CHAPTER XIII

The Opaque Gems
and Ornamental Stones

UNDER the title of this chapter are included an assortment
of gem materials at once inclusive and somewhat hetero-
geneous. On the one hand, we have such familiar gem
stones as turquoise and lapis lazuli, whose rank among jewelry
materials is well established, and on the other, such little known
minerals as rhodonite and malachite, whose use as ornamental
stones is at present entirely confined to materials for carved objects. The possibilities of some of these obscure minerals as applied
to jewelry, especially to modern jewelry forms, would seem to
have been overlooked in the past, and it is hoped that the day is
coming when amazon stone and labradorite will take their place
besides turquoise and lapis lazuli.

THE FELDSPAR GEMS

Among minerals of paramount importance from the point of
view of the vast rock formations which constitute the crust of
our globe, the group of silicate minerals known as the feldspars

shares the first rank with the quartz group described in the two preceding chapters. In contrast with the quartz gems, which, as we have seen, include a rich and varied assemblage of gem varieties, the feldspars do not furnish many species, nor are these of great importance to the jeweler.

Feldspars are all silicates of alumina, the oxide potash entering into composition of the minerals orthoclase and microcline (potash feldspar), and lime and soda combine with alumina and silica to form the oligoclase and labradorite members of the group (lime-soda feldspars). The feldspars are relatively soft, having a hardness of only 6 in the Mohs scale, and are furthermore characterized by two easy cleavages, which are nearly at right angles to each other. The property, however, that is responsible for a great part of the attractiveness characteristic of the feldspar gems is that which causes a twin platy structure in the body of the mineral to reflect light with a milky sheen or with a vivid play of color due to light interference.

MOONSTONE

Two feldspars, oligoclase and a transparent variety of orthoclase called adularia (from the Adular Mountains of Switzerland), often show a milky, blueish opalescence when cut in steep cabochon forms. Because this effect has been compared to the radiance of moonlight, these feldspar gems are known as *moonstones* (see color plate frontispiece). The best stones, that is, those with the most luminous reflections, are now obtained in Ceylon, although formerly beautiful moonstones were furnished by the orthoclase of the St. Gothard district of Switzerland. Moonstones are by far the most popular of the feldspar gems, and in spite of their relative softness, have been used to a limited extent as ring stones. As material for necklace beads, the unique beauty of this gem stone does not seem to be fully appreciated.

A factor that may play some part in the apparent neglect of the possibilities of moonstone is that it is becoming increasingly difficult to obtain suitable gem material even from Oriental sources.

SUNSTONE

An aventurine feldspar, somewhat difficult to distinguish from the quartz aventurine from Russia, described in the preceding chapter, is furnished by the mineral oligoclase. As in the case of the quartz gem, the glittering fire-like reflections are caused by minute included scales; in this case the enclosed mineral is a form of iron oxide (either hematite or goethite), arranged along the cleavage planes of the oligoclase. Aventurine feldspar is usually called *sunstone* in recognition of its red to orange reflections. In Norway, where the best sunstones are to be found, they have long been used by the peasantry for local jewelry, much as cairngorm has been used by the Scotch.

LABRADORITE

The feldspar known as *labradorite* exhibits a remarkable play of color, which originates in the interference of light reflected from thin interior platy surfaces arranged parallel to one of the cleavages. The colors developed range from the blues and greens of a peacock's feather through fine orange and tawny yellow. The home of fine labradorite, as its name suggests, is the Island of St. Paul off the coast of Labrador, and also the coast itself.

AMAZON STONE

An opaque, apple-green variety of the potash feldspar, micro-cline, has been named *Amazon stone* due to an ancient error which supposed the stone to have been first discovered on the Amazon River. As an ornamental stone, the uses of Amazon stone may be said to be confined to such small objects as watch charms and umbrella handles, although recently it has become popular for necklace beads. Originally found in the Ilmen Mountains of Russia, gem Amazon stone has since been procured from many places, among which Pike's Peak in Colorado is famous for large and finely colored stones.

TURQUOISE

There are few gem stones that link together present day usage with the glamor and romance of the past as does the opaque sky blue *turquoise*. Beside the sophisticated jewelry forms in turquoise from the shop windows of Fifth Avenue or Bond Street we can set the marvelous inlaid ornaments made of mosaic-like patterns of turquoise that go back to the time when old Egypt was young. In fact, the earliest group of jewelry forms known in the world, the bracelets of Queen Zer of the first Egyptian dynasty, are set with alternate plaques of cast-gold and carved turquoise.

Turquoise is a complex phosphate of aluminium and copper, with a hardness that is slightly under 6 of the Mohs scale. The blue color, which constitutes the only gem qualification of this stone, is due to the copper present in its composition. Crystals of turquoise are extremely rare; in fact, until quite recently it was thought that this mineral shared with opal the distinction of being the only amorphous gem stone. The quality of being somewhat porous has a distinct influence on the permanence of the clear sky blue color so desirable in this gem stone. The effect of liquids, especially of any dirty or greasy matter, is liable to change the quality of the color from blue to blueish or even yellowish green. From time to time many efforts have been made to render turquoise impervious to moisture, and consequently permanent in color, but hitherto none of these have been markedly successful.

It would seem as though the sources of this popular gem actually linked the distant past with the present. It is true that the most ancient mines on the Sinai peninsula, in which the captive Israelites undoubtedly labored before the advent of Moses, are now no longer productive of turquoise; but on the other hand the deposits near Nishapur in the Persian province of Khorassan are today producing as fine turquoise as they did ten centuries ago. An interesting tradition, indeed, actually connects the old mine known as Isaac's mine near Nishapur with the Hebrew patriarch.

No less ancient are the obscure and vague localities in Russian Turkestan, Afghanistan, Tibet and China which have for ages past supplied to Central Asia the turquoise so highly prized by these Orientals for a host of carved and decorated objects, which so characteristically express their culture.

In North America turquoise is found in the Southwestern United States, in Nevada, California, Arizona and notably in New Mexico. And here again we find abundant evidence that turquoise deposits which have been productive within the memory of the present generation have also furnished the gems which graced aboriginal Americans of great antiquity. Indeed, the prehistoric mines in the Cerrillos district of north-central New Mexico, the most important American sources of turquoise, must have been producing these stones long before Cortez conquered Mexico.

The presence of brownish or yellowish limonite as an associated mineral with the Persian and American turquoise, filling the slender cobwebby cracks traversing the latter mineral, produces a highly pleasing color combination, which is sometimes cut and marketed as *matrix turquoise* or *turquoise matrix* (see color plate frontispiece).

Fossil bones and teeth of extinct animals, when colored blue by iron phosphate, exhibit a certain resemblance to turquoise, but may be readily recognized as distinct from that gem stone by their organic structure as seen under a strong lens. These blue fossil remains are known as *odontolite*, or *bone turquoise*. There are several other opaque stones which somewhat resemble turquoise, of which *chrysocolla*, a copper silicate, is, perhaps, the most easily mistaken for the more precious mineral when cut, but is softer (2 to 4 in hardness), lighter in specific gravity and, in general, more inclined to greenish shades.

Smithsonite, a zinc carbonate, and *calamine*, a zinc silicate, are translucent blueish green minerals, which are occasionally cut into cabochon stones or necklace beads. Their resemblance to turquoise is superficial, and their value as gem material inconsiderable.

LAPIS LAZULI

Hardly less ancient in use or less beautiful in color is the deep ultramarine gem stone known as *lapis lazuli*. So universal was its use in early times that we find engraved cylinder seals and other primitive jewelry forms fashioned from it among Babylonian and Assyrian remains of the very oldest periods. Under the name "sapphire" it appears a number of times in the Old Testament in contexts which indicate a knowledge of it among the Hebrews reaching back to great antiquity.

Although lapis lazuli appears superficially to be homogeneous, it is in reality composed of calcite impregnated and richly colored by three different minerals, all of them silicates of soda and alumina, and all blue in color.

The hardness of this mineral mixture is in the neighborhood of 5 in the Mohs scale, much too soft to be of service for a ring stone, but quite hard enough to fulfill the requirements of the more modern jewelry forms as expressed in beads, pendants and brooches.

Lapis lazuli is essentially an Asiatic gem stone. The Badakshan district of Afghanistan, near the source of the Oxus, contains the oldest and most famous mines, and presumably it was from this source that the lapis lazuli of the ancient world was supplied. Persia, Mesopotamia, Syria and Egypt may all have derived the material for their worked ornaments in lapis lazuli from this center.

The best of the present day lapis lazuli is found near the southern end of Lake Baikal in Siberia, and is known as *Russian lapis* or *Siberian lapis* (see color plate frontispiece).

Apart from the beauty of color, which is a distinguishing characteristic of the Lake Baikal stones, lapis lazuli may be further identified by the presence of small bright yellow metallic grains and veinlets, present in the body of the stones and representing inclusions of iron pyrites.

A deposit of lapis lazuli situated near the town of Ovalle, in the Chilean Andes, furnishes a mottled matrix of inferior color, less valuable than the Russian material.

In addition to the applications to modern jewelry, which are creating a growing demand for lapis lazuli of fine color, this stone has long been a favorite with the Chinese lapidaries for the carving of such characteristic small objects as figurines, pendants and snuff bottles, the material for which comes mainly from the Siberian source.

SODALITE

One of the silicate minerals which combines with others to form lapis lazuli sometimes occurs in grayish blue masses suitable for cut slabs or carved objects. This is *sodalite*, an alumina-soda silicate containing chlorine. In color, sodalite differs slightly but very definitely from lapis lazuli. It is duller in color than the latter, with a tendency toward violet tones. It should be remembered that typical lapis lazuli is the color of the pigment known as ultramarine; in fact, for many years the pigment was made from the powdered stone.

RHODONITE

An opaque ornamental stone of a very characteristic rose-pink color is the manganese silicate, *rhodonite*. This is one of the characteristic Russian decorative stones, which up to the period of the World War was extensively used to express Muscovite taste in small carved objects. Among these should be included trays, small caskets to hold jewels, paper weights and especially the carved eggs which were exchanged among friends at Eastertide, much as we of the West exchange Easter cards.

MALACHITE

Another opaque ornamental stone that is largely associated with the Russian lapidary art of the last century is the green copper carbonate known as *malachite*. The rich, deep grass green of this mineral, mottled as it is with shaded rings much as is agate, is in the opinion of most of us much more attractive than its compatriot, rhodonite.

Both rhodonite and malachite are found in the Ural Mountains in the neighborhood of Ekaterinburg, and were carved in the Imperial Lapidary Works at the latter place into much the same series of objects. Malachite, moreover, has appealed to the Chinese as a medium for carving, and we find many very charming expressions of Chinese lapidary art wrought in this soft but dense and compact medium. There is in China no malachite suitable for carving. All of the Chinese malachite objects are made from Russian material.

AZURITE

Azurite, the dark blue carbonate of copper, is frequently associated with malachite in pleasingly contrasting blue and green patterns.

CHAPTER XIV

*"In ancient times men found the like-
ness of all excellent qualities in jade."*
—CONFUCIUS

CHAPTER XIV

Opaque and Ornamental Stones

JADE

Under the general term *jade* are included massive varieties of at least two mineral species: a massive pyroxene known as *jadeite*, having the composition of a soda-alumina silicate; and a tough, compact amphibole called *nephrite*, corresponding in composition to a lime magnesia-iron silicate. So closely do these mineral materials resemble each other in texture and outward form and color that it is often difficult to distinguish one from the other, especially when carved.

Of the two, jadeite is slightly the harder, having a hardness of 7 in the Mohs scale, as compared with about 6.5 for nephrite. Also the specific gravity of jadeite is rather higher than that of nephrite: 3.34 as compared with about 3.00.

By reason of its toughness and relative hardness, jade was a favorite material for the fashioning of implements employed by primitive man. Wherever jade was obtainable either from a native source or through trade, we find men of the cultural stage corresponding to the late neolithic era employing nephrite, and occasionally jadeite, as materials for celts, axes and other primitive tools and weapons, much as the natives of New Zealand at present make use of their local nephrite.

But, although such jade implements of early man have been found in many places throughout the world, there are but two regions where the use of this material has risen in cultural degree from the purely utilitarian to the decorative stage that places it among the ornamental stones.

In the portions of the tropical Americas including Southern Mexico, Yucatan, Guatemala, Costa Rica, Panama, Colombia, and possibly Ecuador and Peru, the pre-Columbian cultures furnished many carved jade objects of decoration well within the scope of ancient jewelry.

There is now no known deposit of either jadeite or nephrite in these countries. At the time of the conquest of Mexico by Cortez, jade was so rare and so highly esteemed by the Aztecs that it constituted their most precious possession, worth very many times its weight in gold.

It is in China, however, that the high estimation for jade places it above all other gem stones. And it is in China that we find the use of jade not only extending back into vast antiquity, but furnishing us with a means of tracing, through the countless examples of both ancient and modern work in Chinese carved jade, the evolution and development of a highly interesting and extremely attractive expression of the lapidary art.

So closely is the present use of jade identified with China and the Chinese that a description of this ornamental stone may be confined logically to jade as exploited by this people.

As far back as the period of the Chou dynasty in the eleventh century B.C., we find nephrite, presumably imported from Turkestan, Burma or Indo-China, carved into intricate designs, decorated chiefly with geometric motives. Although jade of this early period was originally of some shade of green, corresponding to nephrite as we know it today, the green color has, in many instances, been altered to a brown, ocher or dull red.

This change is purely superficial, affecting only a very thin layer of the surface, and is due to weathering action during long periods of time, the iron oxides which originally colored the stone green or grayish green having been replaced by higher oxides of the ocher to umber shades. Since the oxidizing agencies producing this surface change of color are those which operate best in the upper layers of the soil, it follows that jade pieces that have been buried for long periods of time exhibit it in the highest degree.

With the Han dynasty (B.C. 206 to A.D. 220) much of the geometric formality in jade carving gave way to a freer and more graceful ornamentation. With this stage in the development of Chinese carved jade there grew up a complex symbolism, difficult of interpretation from a Western point of view, and closely interwoven with Taoist and Buddhist myth.

Nephrite from local sources in Shensi and other Chinese provinces, or brought from Eastern Turkestan, or possibly from a deposit near Lake Baikal, furnished most of the jade of this period.

In color the jade from these sources varied from white and gray green to a spinach green, the depth of color increasing with the amount of iron contained in the nephrite. Some jadeite derived from Shensi and Yunnan provinces of China, and from Tibet, was no doubt also used in this, as in the jade work of later periods. It is, however, difficult to separate the jadeite of this culture from nephrite on a basis of color alone, particularly as much of the carvings in both materials has been altered in color through having been buried.

Jade objects belonging to later dynasties, T'ang (618-907),

Sung (960-1280) and Ming (1368-1644), show increased elabo-
ration in carving, and higher relief. This trend culminated in the
highly elaborate carving of the K'ien Lung period (1644-1912),
with its undercut relief, openwork patterns and freer designs. At
this time also the beautiful emerald green jadeite, from the Mogaung district in Upper Burma, began to be imported into China,
and much enriched the materials for Chinese expression in carved
jade. This choicest of the jade varieties is also the best known
to the Western world, under the name of *imperial jade* (see color
plate frontispiece). It is never found in large masses, always in
relatively small areas disseminated through white jadeite, which
fact accounts for the mottled and streaked distribution of color
observable even in some of the finest and most highly prized pieces.

Aside from the semi transparent green of the imperial jade, the
colors which characterize this ornamental stone run the gamut
from the translucent white of "melting snow" or the more opaque
"mutton fat" through various shades of green to deep spinach
color heavily mottled, and even to the black of *chloromelanite*.
Among the rarer colors may be ranked the light chrome yellow
of some Burmese jadeite, a blood red, often met with in patches
in white jadeite, and a still rarer light violet or mauve. A beautiful jadeite from Yunnan province is colored a mottled opaque
green, very like the color of malachite, but differing from the
latter stone in texture.

Although jade ornaments carved in Hindoo, Burman or Siamese
style are met with in these respective countries, these have been
invariably carved in China, or at least by Chinese lapidaries. This
holds true throughout the Orient, the sole exception being the
odd and grotesque figures carved from dark New Zealand nephrite
by the Maories.

Among the mineral substances which more or less resemble

jade, may be included *saussurite*, a greenish or white to gray mineral mixture, composed chiefly of the species zoisite; and *californite*, a compact, translucent, green vesuvianite, sometimes locally called *California jade*.

AGALMATOLITE

Quite apart from these relatively hard substances, and not to be confused in any way with jade, is the highly complex, soapstone-like material variously known as *agalmatolite, figure stone*, or *pagoda stone*. In China more or less crude carvings are wrought in this soft stone, which lends itself to a technique that bears somewhat the same relation to jade that wood carving does to work in the harder ivory. Agalmatolite is ordinarily streaked and mottled in various colors from a greenish-gray of the ground mass to brilliant red and dark chocolate brown. It is so soft that it can be readily cut with a steel tool (knife blade) much as hard wood is cut.

SERPENTINE

Another soft stone that lends itself to a certain kind of decorative carving is *serpentine*, a hydrous magnesium silicate, of wide distribution and often occurring in attractive colors. Although belonging to the monoclinic system of crystallization, serpentine is never found in characteristic monoclinic crystals, its occurrence, in compact and fibrous masses with a waxy luster and a smooth feel, suggesting a resemblance to jade. Its hardness varies from 2.5 to 4 on the Mohs scale, and it is easily scratched by even a soft steel point.

In color, serpentine often develops a rich deep oil green, with considerable mottling in light and dark shading. Serpentine of this color has been fashioned into a number of small carvings, such as trays and cups, by the Russian lapidaries of the last century. Its use is somewhat limited.

SELENITE

Still softer is the fibrous variety of gypsum, the sulphate of calcium, which as *selenite* or *satin spar* was cut to a limited extent in Russia. Such trays and dishes, although not without some attraction due to their silky yellowish sheen, were very fragile, the material being not only soft but very cleavable.

FLUORITE

The fluoride of calcium, variously known as *fluorite, fluorspar* or *fluor*, although brittle and somewhat soft, has been used to some extent for small carved ornaments. A rich purple variety occurring in Derbyshire, England, and locally known as *Derbyshire spar* or as *Blue John*, was formerly made into vases and dishes, which were often turned on a lathe after the manner of wood.

Both purple and green fluorite are skillfully carved by the Chinese. In the case of the purple stone, the material resembles amethyst but may be recognized by its inferior hardness and by the traces of incipient cleavage, which in almost every instance traverse the carved piece.

Green fluorite is of a sea green color suggesting some shades of aquamarine. Both green and purple fluorite are apt to show streaks and patches of lighter tints, or even of a totally different color, as reddish in purple, or Prussian blue in either purple or green. Owing to the very easy octahedral cleavage that characterizes fluorite, carved pieces are very brittle.

An Easter egg carved in the Russian manner from Ural Mountain rhodonite. The rayed cross seen in front is supported on either side by the inscription in Russian letters reading "Christ is risen."

Courtesy of American Museum of Natural History

A figurine representing the "Goddess of Mercy" carved from Tibetan turquoise by a Chinese lapidary.

Courtesy of American Museum of Natural History

A string of beads and gold mounted pendant of Russian lapis lazuli. The latter is carved with the design of the "Mystic Knot." This old string of lapis beads was presented by the late Mrs. Henry Fairfield Osborn to the American Museum.

Courtesy of American Museum of Natural History

A JEWEL CASKET

Made from squares and strips of Russian ornamental stones—rhodonite, agate and jasper.

Courtesy of American Museum of Natural History

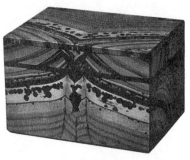

A small jewel casket made from thin matched slabs of malachite. This piece is characteristic of Russian craftsmanship and of the materials used in the 19th Century.

Courtesy of American Museum of Natural History

An irregular slab of Persian turquoise engraved in Arabic characters with a chapter from the Koran Period, about the 15th Century.

Courtesy of American Museum of Natural History

A Chinese carved dish in white jade decorated with the conventionalized mark of long life and five bats symbolizing the five happinesses–long life, health, wealth, love of virtue and a natural death.

Drummond Collection

A FINGERING PIECE

Carved in white jade. This is one of those designs whose smooth rounded contours endear them to the hearts of contemplative Celestials who love to sense their cool, delicious appeal to the sense of touch.

Author's Collection

A large bowl carved with a design of chrysanthemums from spinach green nephrite. This fine carving well represents the work of the Chinese jade carvers of the last century.

Courtesy of American Museum of Natural History

CHAPTER XV

"I beheld also in the midst of this above men-
tioned stream an abundance of various kinds of
jewels and minerals."
—Sixth Voyage of Es-Sindbad of the Sea
(Arabian Nights)

Unusual Gem Stones

U NDER this heading are included a number of gem minerals which, owing either to their softness or to the difficulty of obtaining suitable material for cutting, have not found their way into general use.

ANATASE

This oxide of titanium is also called *octahedrite* in recognition of the shape of its crystals, which are square pyramids. Transparent varieties are occasionally cut as facetted gems, yielding brown stones of a high index of refraction and varying from 5.5 to 6 in hardness.

ANDALUSITE

A silicate of alumina which has rarely been cut. The step cut or brilliant cut stones are brown or green in color, somewhat resembling tourmalines, and show considerable dichroism. Although named for the Province of Andalusia in Spain, gem *andalusites* are found principally in Ceylon and in Minas Geraes, Brazil. An opaque variety containing black carbonaceous inclusions and known as *chiastrolite* is sometimes polished to show the cross shaped and tessellated patterns.

APATITE

Transparent varieties of this calcium phosphate have, in rare instances, been cut into gem stones, yielding green, blue and violet step cut or brilliant cut gems. The hardness of *apatite* is only 5, much too soft for a practical stone.

AXINITE

This boro-silicate of lime and alumina is sometimes found in transparent varieties, which yield small clove-brown, honey-yellow, and violet-brown cut stones. These are characterized by strong pleochroism, and by a hardness slightly under that of quartz. Cut stones of *axinite* are very rare.

BENITOITE

This newly discovered (1907) gem mineral bid fair in the first decade of this century to rise to the importance of at least a semi-precious stone. The scarcity of gem material at the sole place where it has been found, however, has prevented it from being popular or, in fact, at all widely known. *Benitoite* takes its name from its home—San Benito County, California. It occurs in trigonal pyramidal crystals of a color closely resembling the sapphires from Ceylon and Montana, and of a hardness of 6 to 6.50 of the Mohs scale. The pleochroism of benitoite in the deep colored stones is very intense, the color varying from deep blue to white, depending on the direction in which light travels in the stone. Benitoite is a barium titano-silicate.

BERYLLONITE

The soda-beryllium phosphate of this name is rare among minerals. The small, clear, colorless crystals are very seldom found in sizes which would yield stones as large as 2 carats. The largest and clearest crystals come from Maine. As a gem stone, *beryllonite* may be regarded as negligible.

CASSITERITE

The few stones that have been cut from transparent crystals of this oxide of tin are yellow to reddish in color, with a high index of refraction and color dispersion. Light colored stones are brilliant and have considerable fire. The hardness, which is below that of quartz, prevents the use of *cassiterite* in jewelry. It is somewhat of a curio among gems.

CHLORASTROLITE

This hydrous silicate, which is found in mottled, greenish, fibrous aggregates, weathered out in the form of small pebbles from the rocks around Isle Royale, on the Michigan shore of Lake Superior, is sometimes locally made into cabochon stones of some attractiveness. It is soft and easily worked.

CYANITE

The bladed triclinic crystals of this alumina silicate have been occasionally cut into small stepped stones. These are blue to grayish blue in color, soft and not always transparent.

DIOPSIDE

The only mineral species, other than jadeite, among the numerous and widely distributed group of the monoclinic pyroxenes that has gem stone possibilities is this lime-magnesia silicate. Attractive yellowish green stones, not unlike some peridots in color, have been cut from *diopside* crystals, especially from an occurrence at Dekalb, New York. Although softer than peridot, there seems to be no valid reason why these gem stones should not enjoy more than the merely local reputation which is now accorded to them.

ENSTATITE
Another member of the pyroxene group (an orthorhombic pyroxene), this mineral is the victim of a popular misnomer. It is known in South Africa, where as small green transparent crystals it accompanies the diamonds, as *green garnet*. Brilliant cut stones are cut and sold locally.

EUCLASE
Only the rarity of this silicate of aluminium and beryllium prevents it from ranking with aquamarine, to which gem stone it bears a close resemblance. Occurring very infrequently with the topaz deposits of Minas Novas, in the province of Minas Geraes, Brazil, the blue to sea-green crystals of *euclase* are so small and command such a high price that their jewelry use is completely eclipsed by the cheaper blue topaz and aquamarine.

HEMATITE AND RUTILE
Certain compact varieties of *hematite*, the sesquioxide of iron, and of *rutile*, an oxide of titanium, yield, on being polished, opaque stones of a black color and a high metallic luster, which latter may be compared with gun metal. These stones have a limited jewelry use, principally for mourning jewelry. They are usually cut cabochon, or in round beads and pear shapes.

HIDDENITE

Another American gem stone, which, like benitoite, never attained popularity because of the lack of suitable material, is *hiddenite*, a variety of spodumene, a silicate of aluminium and lithium. The fine green color of this stone is described in the name *lithia emerald* which is sometimes given to it. Hiddenite was discovered in 1881 in Alexander County, North Carolina, by Mr. W. E. Hidden, in honor of whom it was named. The gem crystals are small, seldom yielding stones over one carat. No other source of hiddenite is known.

IOLITE

This silicate of magnesium, aluminium and iron is better known as *water-sapphire* (saphir d'eau) because water worn masses and crystals are to be found among the stream gravels of Ceylon. These are smoky blue in color, with considerable dichroism (smoky blue and yellowish white), which latter characteristic accounts for another name—*dichroite*—which has been given to this gem stone. *Iolite* is also found near Guilford, Connecticut. The small but attractive stones made from iolite are usually stepcut. Their popularity, which is largely a thing of the past, was mostly confined to the Continent of Europe and to the nineteenth century.

KUNZITE

Unlike the other gem stones described in this chapter, this semi-precious variety of spodumene at present enjoys a considerable degree of popularity. Its color, which is a light lilac red, sometimes described as wisteria pink, might be confused with morganite (Chapter VII) and rubellite (Chapter IX). But apart from the distinction that *kunzite* is strongly dichroic, it will be found by comparison that its unique color is also distinctive. Kunzite was discovered in 1903 in Pala, San Diego County, California. It was named in honor of Dr. George F. Kunz, the well known gem expert, who first called attention to its possibilities as a gem stone. Gem crystals yielding perfect stones up to 200 carats have been found. Although essentially an American gem stone, kunzite has also been found in fine gem crystals in Madagascar.

PHENACITE

This clear, colorless silicate of beryllium has been known to yield stones similar in appearance to those of rock crystal. It is found associated with beryl gem stones in the Ural Mountains, and in Minas Geraes, Brazil. Stones cut from *phenacite* do not differ from rock crystal gems and are much more expensive.

PREHNITE

Soft, translucent, pale oil-green and sea-green stones have been cut from this lime-alumina silicate. These are but little known outside of the neighborhood of the deposit which produces them. For instance, Paterson, New Jersey, has yielded some finely colored *prehnite* specimens, but very few of them are suitable for cutting into cabochon shapes.

PYRITE

This hard sulphide of iron (hardness 6.5, Mohs scale) has occasionally been cut to furnish metallic brass yellow stones. These have little beauty and exist largely as local curiosities among gem stones.

SPHALERITE

Transparent varieties of this sulphide of zinc are sometimes

cut, yielding soft orange to yellow stones of a high index of refraction. Unfortunately it is almost impossible to find perfectly
clear *sphalerite*, even at Santander, Spain, a notable locality for
the variety.

TITANITE

The titano-silicate of calcium, also called *sphene*, furnishes in
its transparent varieties beautiful gems. These clear green, yellow and brownish stones rival the diamond in brilliancy and fire,
but are too soft to stand the wear of ring stones and have too
easy a cleavage to make satisfactory pendant or brooch stones.
It seems indeed unfortunate that gem stones possessed of such
attractions in the show case cannot be worn with safety. The
source of the clearest stones is the St. Gothard district of Switzerland.

THOMSONITE

Pebbles of this hydrated calcium, sodium and aluminium silicate are to be found associated with chlorastrolite on the Michigan shore of Lake Superior. These exhibit an attractive white,
red, green and yellow mottling, and are cut cabochon and distributed locally.

VARISCITE

This apple-green to blueish green hydrated aluminium phosphate resembles turquoise in everything but color. The attractive
contrast between the pale green of the rounded *variscite* nodules
and their matrix of light brown or gray has led to the local distribution of this stone under the name *Amatrice* (*American
matrix*). Its occurrence is confined to Central Utah.

VESUVIANITE

Stones cut from this silicate of aluminium and calcium are very rare. They are transparent, leaf-green and yellowish brown in color, somewhat resembling tourmaline and zircon. They are readily distinguishable from either of these latter gem stones by the absence of dichroism (for tourmaline) or of double refraction (for zircon). Gem varieties come from Russia, and from Piedmont and Mount Vesuvius in Italy.

CHAPTER XVI

"The bone of the gods turned into pearl, that animated, dwells in the waters. That do I fasten upon thee unto life, luster, strength, longevity, unto life lasting a hundred autumns. May the amulet of pearl protect thee!"
—HYMNS OF THE ATHORVAVEDA

CHAPTER XVI

Organic Products Used as Gems

MATERIALS which come under the heading of this chapter do not conform to the definition of gem stones; in fact, they are in no sense minerals. Because, however, they have from ancient times been used in jewelry, and because one of them, the pearl, is ranked among the precious gems, it is highly appropriate to add them to the products of nature included in this book.

PEARL

In spite of the fact that the perishable character of *pearls* as compared with mineral gems prevent us from actually connecting them with the very ancient races of men, we still have considerable evidence that the lustrous beauty of these products of the sea appealed strongly to the decorative sense of primitive man. It seems probable that pearls were strung as beads at a period at least as early as were pieces of turquoise or carnelian, and it is possible that as gems they may have antedated turquoise and carnelian. Pearls have continued to rank high among the precious possessions of all races of men from that early day to the present.

Pearls are composed of a substance identical with the iridescent lining of some shells, mother of pearl or nacre, interspersed in alternate layers with calcium carbonate. The horny organic matter is known as conchiolin, and the calcium carbonate is of the kind called aragonite. The formation of this product of the pearl-bearing mollusk is due to abnormal conditions affecting its life history. Any mollusk, whether of the bivalve or univalve type, which possesses a nacreous shell, has the power of producing pearls when irritated by the intrusion within its shell of some foreign matter. This intruder which disturbs the comfort of the oyster, mussel or clam may be a boring parasite, a worm, a small fish or even a grain of sand. The mollusk proceeds to rid itself of the irritation of the foreign substance by covering it with successive layers of carbonate of lime and nacre, the layers, of course, being extremely thin and the outermost one consisting of nacre. In this way are built up the round, oval, pear shaped or irregular forms of pearls.

Not every pearl formed in this way is valuable, and a number of kinds are not particularly attractive. The beautiful and costly pearls are formed by a species of oyster, called *Pinctada margaritifera*, inhabiting the warm waters of the tropical seas. Such pearls are called *Oriental pearls* and are characterized by a shimmering luster from below the surface caused by the effect of reflected and refracted light from the various layers, of much the same kind which, as we have seen in the case of the opal or the moonstone, rendered these stones so beautiful. Jewelers speak of this luster characteristic of Oriental pearls as "orient." In color Oriental pearls are usually white, although such faint tints as yellowish and blueish are not uncommon, and the rarer salmon-pink, reddish and gray are sometimes encountered. Black pearls are rare and valuable, but *not*, as is frequently stated, of more value than the finest white gems.

The pearl fisheries of the Persian Gulf, off the coast of Arabia, have been famous since very early times, and still produce most of the Oriental pearls. The Gulf of Manaar adjacent to the coast of Ceylon is noted for the beautiful white and silvery pearls to be found in a small oyster which inhabits these waters.

The waters of the Pacific are productive of pearl oysters off the coasts of Northern and Western Australia and near certain islands of the South Pacific. In the tropical waters off the Western Continent pearl mollusks are found off Venezuela, as well as adjacent to the famous Pearl Islands, which lie almost at the Pacific entrance of the Panama Canal. Fine black pearls come from the Pacific coast of Mexico, and especially along the coast of Lower California.

CULTURED PEARLS

Recently the pearl oysters that flourish in Japanese waters have been induced to produce pearls by means of the deliberate introduction of a foreign substance. Such stimulated pearl productions are called *cultured pearls*. They were at first grown on the shell of the oyster by the simple expedient of slipping a small shell bead into the partly opened shell. This method produced only "half pearls," since the cultivated growth had to be cut away from the shell to which it was attached. As an improvement on this method, the shell (mother of pearl) bead is now placed in a sac formed by making a small incision in the fleshy part of the oyster, and thus insuring the round surface of superposed layers with which the oyster surrounds it. Three to five years are required to make a cultured pearl, during which time the oysters repose in specially prepared beds laid down in proper depth of sea water.

FRESH WATER PEARLS

Fresh water mussels of the species known as *Unio margarita* abound in many of the rivers and fresh water lakes of the United States, and especially in the valley of the Upper Mississippi. These mollusks secrete a nacre and produce pearls, which, although less valuable than Oriental pearls, often display a luster and color which render them highly attractive.

A conch shell mollusk inhabiting the waters in the neighborhood of the Florida Keys produces a somewhat opaque and porcelain-like pink or yellowish pearl. Such pearls, known as *conch pearls*, are of relatively little value. Still lower in the scale of values are the pearly secretions produced by clams and edible oysters of the northern Atlantic coast. Like the conch pearls these latter have much the luster and opaqueness of china.

The standard of weight for pearls is the pearl grain, equal to one-fourth of a carat. In estimating values, a number of factors must be considered, such as "orient," color, and shape. The foundation value for a one grain pearl of a certain quality, arrived at through the consideration of these various factors, is termed the *base* and furnishes a standard for the valuation of larger pearls. The values for pearls of various weights are reckoned in terms of the square of the weight multiplied by the base. A two grain pearl is worth four times a one grain one of the same quality.

Because pearls are soft and easily scratched, care is necessary to preserve their luster unimpaired. Once dulled by wear, the luster of a fine pearl is almost impossible of restoration, although attempts are sometimes made to remove the worn skin and expose the fresh layer underneath. Such a delicate operation, it is needless to say, is difficult even in the hands of one skilled in such restorations. It is said that pearls lose their luster and become "dead" when laid away for long periods, and that it is necessary to wear them in order to retain their beauty. It is also assumed, on good evidence, that certain people can, by wearing pearls, restore their lost luster better than can others. All this seems to indicate that in the wearing of pearls a certain amount of bodily moisture prevents the layers of nacre and aragonite from separating through dryness and consequently prevents the loss of orient which would occur if they were not so imperceptibly moistened.

AMBER

Scarcely secondary to the pearl in the matter of antiquity of use is the fossil tree gum known to us as *amber*. Although not a direct product of the sea, amber has an intimate association with it, since it is washed up by the waves in various parts of the world.

Not only were strings of rough amber beads worn by men and women in prehistoric times, but these same strings of amber beads constituted important articles of ancient commerce and in all probability were also used as a means of exchange. Homer refers to amber as being traded by the Phoenicians (Odyssey, XV, 460), which explains why we find Baltic amber in the possession of so many and such widely separated ancient peoples.

Amber differs from other hardened resinous tree gums mainly in its extreme age. Whether or not such products as the Kauri gum of New Zealand or the copal gum of Africa would become amber after a lapse of forty or fifty million years, we have no means of knowing. Incredibly old as true amber is according to our standards of time, it still bears the proofs that it was once soft and sticky in the presence of certain insects, flies, gnats and mosquitoes imprisoned in it. Caught up in the viscous sap of coniferous trees of the Oligocene epoch some forty-five million years ago, much as a modern fly might be in present day spruce gum, these extinct insects tell their own story about what was happening in their time.

As might be expected, amber differs widely in color with the localities furnishing it. All of it is soft, with a hardness of only 2.5 in the Mohs scale. It is also relatively light in weight, only slightly heavier than water. But light as true amber is, some of the more recent gums are even lighter, so that it is possible to make a brine by dissolving common salt in water that will cause Kauri or even copal gum to float, while true amber will sink. This is a simple and reliable test to distinguish old fossil amber from a more recent gum.

The amber from the vicinity of Königsberg in East Prussia, known as *Baltic amber*, is by far the best known variety of this organic substance. In color this amber ranges from light canary yellow to a yellowish-orange, and its translucency varies from perfectly transparent to clouded opaque. Up to about the middle of the last century all Baltic amber was recovered from the sea, a flotsam product gathered at low tide, and often entangled with sea weed. About 1860, however, exploration showed deposits of amber underground not far inshore from the coast, and much of the amber that is now cut into beads, pipe stems, cigarette holders and small objects is mined from these East Prussia deposits.

Darker, richer in color and more consistently transparent is the amber that is washed up on the shores of Sicily in the neighborhood of Catania. *Sicilian amber* is mostly of a rich reddish brown color, sometimes exhibiting a blue or green fluorescence. The latter is a reflection from the interior of the mass rather than a body color, and may be compared to the reflected color seen when certain heavy oils are poured in a brilliant sunlight. Sicilian amber is more highly prized than Baltic amber, and is now somewhat difficult to obtain. The fluorescent variety is now very rare.

A small deposit of somewhat inferior amber occurs in Roumania and is locally used for small ornaments. Very little of it, however, finds its way out of the country.

Throughout the southeast of Asia small carved amber ornaments and objects of art are to be met with. These are executed in a highly attractive kind of amber mined in the Naga Hills of Upper Burma, not far from the locality for imperial jade mentioned in Chapter XIV. The color of *Burmese amber* is very variable, running the gamut of shades from deep red through brown to clear honey yellow, besides which, many variations of clearness and opacity are encountered in this variety, including a rare black amber.

Imitations of amber are fairly easy of fabrication from celluloid, bakelite or Canada balsam. None of these will become electrified by friction as will amber.

Kauri gum has been used to imitate Burmese amber, especially when stained red, its normal color being a somewhat dead light yellow resembling lemon jelly. In addition to the gravity test in brine, already mentioned, Kauri gum is distinguishable by being more soluble in alcohol than is true amber. A drop of alcohol will cause a certain stickiness to develop on the surface of Kauri gum, whereas several moments are required for a similar effect to appear on the surface of an amber piece.

Amber is fusible at a relatively low heat, a fact which is taken advantage of by the workers in Baltic amber to fuse scraps of amber in air tight iron boxes, producing cakes of clear reconstructed amber or "amberoid." When cut, and possibly stained to imitate Burmese amber, this substitute is very difficult to distinguish from mined amber.

CORAL

Like pearl, *coral* is a product of sea life. It is secreted by minute sea organisms known as coral polyps, and is composed mainly of calcium carbonate. The variety employed as a gem is a red to pink variety, sometimes called *precious coral*. This red coral is found in Mediterranean waters off the coasts of Tunisia, Algeria, Morocco, Sardinia, Corsica, France and Naples, at which latter city much of it is carved into necklace, bracelet and rosary beads.

A somewhat similar red coral occurs near the Island of Formosa in the China Sea, and is carved into small decorative objects and figurines by Chinese artists.

SHELL

The helmet-like shell of a large mollusk found in the West Indian waters and off the coast of Madagascar has frequently been used as material for cameo carving in high relief. The outer white layer of the shell is used for the design, and the sepia brown body layer for the contrasting background.

The art of cutting shell cameos is a comparatively modern one and originated in Italy in the fifteenth and sixteenth centuries. Shell cameos are cut almost exclusively in Florence.

An elaborately carved circular panel screen of spinach green nephrite showing a design of dragons and clouds. Also mounted in the teak wood base are two white jade panel insets showing other phases of Chinese carving in jade.

Courtesy of American Museum of Natural History

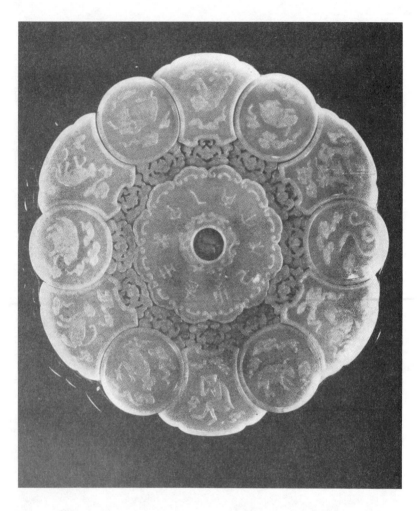

A masterpiece of modern carving in white jade was selected for this gift to a famous emperor–Kien Lung. The central piece has a loose button decorated with the yang yin (universal life symbol). Surrounding the central piece are twelve pieces fitted together, each of which is carved with a representation of one of the twelve creatures which in China correspond to the signs of the zodiac as used by Westerners.

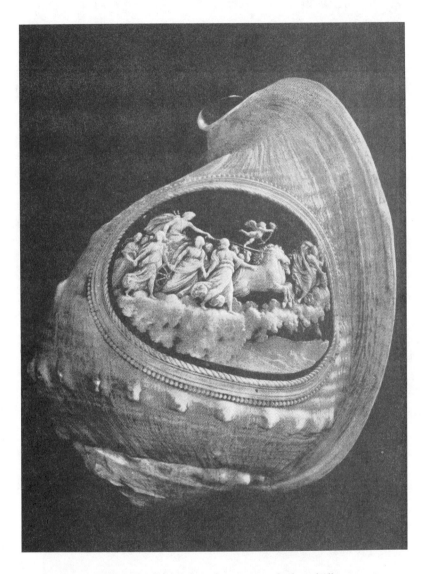

A West Indian helmet shell, showing the way in which a shell cameo is executed from the differently colored layers of these shells.

The dragons on this jade cup are of the form which developed in China in the Ming dynasty. The perfection in carving, however, shows the piece to be of later date, probably early Kien Lung.

Drummond Collection

A dress ornament carved with a dragon design in low relief from Burmese amber. Chinese carving.

Courtesy of American Museum of Natural History

LIST OF BOOKS
ON GEMS

BABELON, ERNEST
Catalogue des Camées antique et modern de la
Bibliotheque nationale.
  2 vols. Paris, 1897.

BARBOT, CH.
Traité complet des pierres précieuses.
  Paris, 1858.

BAUER, MAX
Edelsteinkunde.
  Leipzig, 1900.

  SPENCER, L. J.
  Translation of the above.
    London (no date).

  SCHEOSSMACHER
  Revision of above.
    Leipzig, 1932.

BERQUEM, ROBERT DE
Traité des pierres précieuses.
  Paris, 1669.

BURNHAM, S. M.
Precious Stones in Nature, Art and Literature.
  Boston, 1886.

CATELLE, W. R.
Precious Stones.
  Philadelphia and London, 1903.

CATELLE, W. R.
The Pearl, its Story, its Charm and its Value.
  Philadelphia and London, 1907.

CATELLE, W. R.
The Diamond.
  New York, 1911.

CHURCH, A. H.
Precious Stones.
  London, 1913.

[191]

CLAREMONT, LEOPOLD
  The Gem Cutter's Craft.
  London, 1906.

COOPER, C. W.
  The Precious Stones of the Bible.
  1924.

ESCARD, JEAN
  Les Pierres Précieuses.
  Paris, 1914.

EMANUEL, H.
  Diamonds and Precious Stones.
  London, 1865.

FARRINGTON, O. C.
  Gems and Gem Minerals.
  Chicago, 1903.

GROTH, P.
  Grundriss der Edelsteinkunde.
  Leipzig, 1887.

HAMLIN, A. C.
  The Tourmaline.
  Boston, 1873.

HAÜY, RÉNÉ JUST
  Traité des caractères physique des pierres précieuses pour servir à
  leur détermination lorsqu' elles ont été taillées.
  Paris, 1817.

HOWARD, J. HARRY
  Handbook for the Amateur Lapidary.
  Greenville, S. C., 1935.

JACQUEMART, J.
  Les gemmes et joyaux de la Couronne.
  2 vols. Paris, 1886.

JEFFRIES, DAVID
  Treatise on Diamonds.
  London, 1750.

KRAUS, E. H. AND HOLDEN, E. F.
Gems and Minerals.
New York, 1931.

KUNZ, G. F.
Gems and Precious Stones of North America.
New York, 1890.

KUNZ, G. F.
History of the Gems found in North Carolina.
Bull. 12 N. Carolina Geol. Survey, 1907.

KUNZ, G. F.
The Curious Lore of Precious Stones. (Dover reprint)
New York and Philadelphia, 1913.

KUNZ, G. F.
The Magic of Jewels and Charms. (Dover reprint)
New York and Philadelphia, 1915.

KUNZ, G. F.
Rings for the Finger.
New York and Philadelphia, 1917.

KUNZ, G. F. AND STEVENSON
The Book of the Pearl. (Dover reprint)
New York, 1908.

MAWE, JOHN
A Treatise on Diamonds and Precious Stones.
London, 1823.

OSBORNE, DUFFIELD
Engraved Gems.
New York, 1912.

POGUE, JOSEPH E.
The Turquoise.
Memoirs National Academy of Science.
Vol. XII, Part II, 1915.

RESENTHAL, LEONARD
The Kingdom of the Pearl.
New York and London (no date).

RICHTER, GISELA, M. A.
  Catalogue of Engraved Gems of the Classical Style.
  Metropolitan Museum, 1920.

ROTHSCHILD, M. D.
  Precious Stones.
  New York, 1889.

SMITH, G. F. HERBERT
  Gem Stones and their Distinctive Characters.
  London, 1919.

STREETER, E. W.
  The Great Diamonds of the World.
  London, 1882.

STREETER, EDWIN W.
  Precious Stones and Gems.
  London, 1884.

TAVERNIER, JEAN BAPTISTE
  Voyage en Turquie, en Perse et Aux Indes.
  Paris, 1676.

WADE, FRANK B.
  Diamonds, A Study of the Factors that Govern their Value.
  New York and London, 1916.

WADE, FRANK B.
  A Text Book of Precious Stones for the Jewelers
  and the Gem Loving Public.
  New York and London, 1918.

WODISKA, J.
  A Book of Precious Stones.
  1909.

WOLLASTON, T. C.
  Opal, The Gem of the "Never Never."
  1924.

DESCRIPTIVE TABLES

OF

GEMS

✳

Name and Mineral Composition	Page	Color	Transparency	Hardness = H Specific Gravity = G	Occurrence	Usual Cutting
AGATE A gel variety of quartz	145	Banded in sepia and sienna	Translucent	H = 7 G = 2.65	Uruguay, Brazil—cut in Idar, Germany	Ornamental carvings
ALEXANDRITE A variety of chrysoberyl	125	Green by daylight, red by artificial light	Transparent	H = 8.5 G = 3.64	Russia (finest), Ceylon	Brilliant
ALMANDINE A variety of garnet iron-aluminium silicate	107	Fine deep crimson	Transparent	H = 7 G = 4.09	Burma, India, Ceylon, Madagascar	Combination brilliant step, cabochon
AMAZON STONE A variety of microcline, a potash feldspar	153	Robin's egg green	Opaque	H = 6 G = 2.56	Russia, Colorado, Virginia	Cabochon stones and carved objects
AMBER A fossil tree gum	185	Yellow, brown Reddish brown	Transparent Translucent	H = 2.5 G = 1.09	East Prussia, Sicily, Roumania, Burma	Cabochon, beads, ornamental carvings
AMETHYST A variety of crystalline quartz	135	Light to dark purple	Transparent	H = 7 G = 2.65	Russia, Brazil, Maine, Pennsylvania	Combination brilliant-step cut
ANDRADITE A variety of garnet calcium-iron silicate	108	Shades of yellow to bright emerald-green = Demantoid	Transparent	H = 7 G = 3.78	Piedmont, Italy, Russia	Brilliant and combination brilliant-step
AQUAMARINE A variety of beryl, alumina-beryllium silicate	96	Sea green varying to blueish	Transparent	H = 7.5 to 8 G = 2.66 2.68	Russia, Brazil, Ceylon, Maine, North Carolina	Step cut and combination brilliant-step cut
AVENTURINE A variety of quartz inclosing mica	143	Leek green and golden-reddish	Translucent	H = 7 G = 2.65	Ural Mountains, India	Ornamental carvings
AZURITE A carbonate of copper	159	Deep pure blue	Opaque	H = 3.5 G = 3.7 to 3.8	Arizona, Ural Mountains, Rhodesia	Combined with malachite, it is cut cabochon
BERYL GEMS Includes q.v. EMERALD AQUAMARINE MORGANITE	194					
BLOODSTONE A gel variety of quartz	147	Dark green with red spots and streaks	Opaque	H = 7 G = 2.65	Ural Mountains, India	Ornamental carvings

Name and Mineral Composition	Page	Color	Transparency	Hardness = H Specific Gravity = G	Occurrence	Usual Cutting
CAIRNGORM OR SMOKY QUARTZ A crystalline variety of quartz	136	Smoky gray to smoky brown	Transparent	H = 7 G = 2.65	Widely distributed— Scotland, Switzerland, Dauphiny, Colorado	Combination brilliant-step cut, also for carved objects
CARNELIAN A gel variety of quartz	144	Orange red	Translucent	H = 7 G = 2.65	Ural Mountains, India, Brazil	Ornamental carvings
CHALCEDONY A gel variety of quartz	143	White to bluish gray	Translucent	H = 7 G = 2.65	Ural Mountains, Uruguay, Transylvania	Ornamental carvings
CHRYSOBERYL Beryllium aluminate; see also Alexandrite Cymophane	123	Pure yellow shading to various tones of green	Transparent	H = 8.5 G = 3.5 to 3.8	Brazil, Ceylon	Brilliant, brilliant-step, cabochon
CHRYSOCOLLA Copper silicate	156	Sky blue to greenish	Translucent to opaque	H = 2 to 4 G = 2.4	Universally distributed in copper mining regions	Cabochon
CHRYSOPHRASE A gel variety of quartz	144	Apple green	Translucent	H = 7 G = 2.65	Silesia, Arizona, California	Cabochon and ornamental carvings
CITRINE A variety of crystallized quartz	136	Light yellow to smoky yellow	Transparent	H = 7 G = 2.65	Spain, Scotland, Germany	Brilliant-step cut
CORAL, Organic carbonate of lime	188	White, pink to reddish (ox blood)	Opaque	H = 3.5 G = 2.7	Mediterranean coastal countries, Formosa	Beads, small ornamental carvings
CORUNDUM GEMS Aluminium oxide; see under Ruby, Sapphire	90					
CYANITE, ALSO KYANITE Aluminium silicate	173	Grayish blue to sky blue	Transparent to translucent	H = 4 to 7 varying with direction G = 3.5 to 3.7	Switzerland, Tyrol	Small step-cut stones
CYMOPHANE A variety of chrysoberyl	124	Yellowish to yellowish green	Transparent with cat's eye effect = Oriental cat's eye	H = 8.5 G = 3.7	Ceylon	Cabochon

[197]

Name and Mineral Composition	Page	Color	Transparency	Hardness = H Specific Gravity = G	Occurrence	Usual Cutting
DIAMOND Crystallized carbon	67	Clear, colorless, but sometimes faintly colored as yellow, brown; rarely green, red, blue	Transparent	H = 10 G = 3.5	South Africa, Rhodesia, Congo, Brazil	Brilliant
DIOPSIDE A variety of pyroxene calcium-magnesium silicate	173	Yellowish green	Transparent	H = 6 G = 3.3	Piedmont, Italy, Tyrol, Ontario, New York	Brilliant or brilliant-step cut
EMERALD A variety of beryl	94	Fine grass green	Transparent	H = 8 G = 2.71	Colombia, Ural Mountains, North Carolina	Step cut
ESSONITE OR HESSONITE A variety of garnet, calcium-aluminium silicate	108	Orange yellow to cinnamon brown	Transparent	H = 6 G = 3.53	Ceylon (sometimes called Hyacinth), Piedmont, Italy	Brilliant-step cut—sometimes engraved as cameos and intaglios
FELDSPAR GEMS See under Amazon Stone Moonstone	151					
FLUORITE Calcium fluoride	168	Sea green to blue, purple, often variegated	Translucent	H = 4 G = 3.18	England, also widely distributed	Ornamental carvings
GARNET GEMS See under Almandine, Andradite, Essonite, Pyrope, Rhodolite, Spessartite	106					
HYACINTH A variety of zircon, zirconium silicate; see also under Essonite	117	Aurora-red to violet-red	Transparent	H = 7 G = 4.67 to 4.7	France, Ilmen Mountains, Ceylon	Brilliant
INDICOLITE A variety of tourmaline, aluminium boro-silicate	114	Indigo blue	Transparent	H = 7 to 7.5 G = 2.9 to 3.2	Brazil, Maine	Brilliant-step cut, step cut
JACINTH A variety of zircon, zirconium silicate	117	Leaf green, yellow, orange and smoky orange	Transparent	H = 7.25 G = 4.0 to 4.1	Ceylon, Siam, Australia, S. Africa	Brilliant

Name and Mineral Composition	Page	Color	Transparency	Hardness = H Specific Gravity = G	Occurrence	Usual Cutting
JADE See under Jadeite, Nephrite	163					
JADEITE A massive variety of pyroxene, sodium-aluminium silicate	163	Apple green to greenish white, often white spotted green, also red, yellow, mauve and deep green	Translucent	H = 6.5 to 7 G = 3.3 to 3.5	Burma, Kashmir, Tibet, Yu-nan, China	Ornamental Chinese carved objects
JASPER A gel variety of quartz	147	Brown, red, yellow, green, gray	Opaque	H = 7 G = 2.65	Universal distribution —Russia, India, Egypt, Brazil, western U.S.A.	Carved ornamental objects, beads
KUNZITE A variety of spodumene, lithium-aluminium silicate	175	Lavender-pink, wisteria-violet	Transparent	H = 6.5 to 7 G = 3.1 to 3.2	California, Madagascar	Brilliant, brilliant-step cut
LABRADORITE A lime-soda feldspar	153	Gray with brilliant reflected play of color, green, yellow, orange, blue	Translucent	H = 6 G = 2.65 to 2.7	Island of St. Paul, Labrador	Small carved objects
LAPIS LAZULI A complex silicate	156	Ultramarine blue	Opaque	H = 5 to 5.5 G = 2.4	Afghanistan, Siberia, Chile	Ornamental carvings, chiefly Chinese
MALACHITE Copper carbonate	158	Grass green	Opaque	H = 3.5 G = 3.7 to 4	Universal distribution —Suitable material from Siberia, West Africa, Arizona	Ornamental carvings
MOONSTONE A potassium feldspar, potassium-aluminium silicate	152	White to light blueish-gray with luminescence	Translucent	H = 6 G = 2.57	Ceylon, Switzerland	Cabochon, beads
MORGANITE A variety of beryl, beryllium-aluminium silicate	90	Rose pink	Transparent	H = 7.5 G = 2.74	California, Madagascar	Brilliant-step cut
NEPHRITE A massive amphibole, calcium-magnesium-iron silicate (included under jade)	163	White, various shades of green, gray-green, leaf-green, spinach-green to black	Translucent	H = 6.5 G = 2.9 to 3.1	China, Tibet, Siberia, Russia, Silesia, New Zealand, Alaska	Ornamental carvings, chiefly Chinese

[199]

Name and Mineral Composition	Page	Color	Transparency	Hardness = H Specific Gravity = G	Occurrence	Usual Cutting
ONYX A gel variety of quartz	146	Black and white quartz in alternate bandings	Translucent to opaque	H = 7 G = 2.65	India	Cabochon, also engraved cameos and intaglios
OPAL A gel form of hydrated silica	126	White and black with internal play of color. Also reddish (*fire opal*)	Translucent	H = 6 G = 2.15	Mexico, Czecho-slovakia, Australia, Nevada	Cabochon
PERIDOT A variety of chrysolite, iron-magnesium silicate	118	Olive green	Transparent	H = 6.5 G = 3.4	Zebirget (Red Sea), Upper Burma, Queens-land, Arizona, New Mexico	Step cut, brilliant-step
PYROPE A variety of garnet, magnesium-aluminium silicate	107	Deep, brilliant red	Transparent	H = 7.25 G = 3.5 to 3.7	South Africa, Bohemia, Arizona, N. Mexico	Brilliant
QUARTZ GEMS Oxide of Silicon See under Agate Citrine Amethyst Jasper Aventurine Onyx Bloodstone Rock Crystal Cairngorm Rose Quartz Chalcedony Smoky Quartz	131-147					
RHODOLITE A variety of garnet, iron-magnesium-alumi-nium silicate	107	Violet red	Transparent	H = 7 G = 3.84	N. Carolina, Ceylon	Brilliant
RHODONITE Manganese silicate	158	Light brownish red to rose pink	Opaque	H = 6 G = 3.67	Russia, Sweden, Mas-sachusetts, New Jersey	Ornamental carved objects, mostly Russian workmanship
ROCK CRYSTAL A crystalline variety of quartz	132	Colorless, water-clear	Transparent	H = 7 G = 2.66	Universally distributed —Brazil, Switzerland, Japan	Ornamental carved objects, beads, crystal balls
ROSE QUARTZ A crystalline variety of quartz	137	Pink	Translucent	H = 7 G = 2.66	Ural Mountains, Bavaria, Maine, S. Dakota	Ornamental carved objects, mostly Chinese workmanship

Name and Mineral Composition	Page	Color	Transparency	Hardness = H Specific Gravity = G	Occurrence	Usual Cutting
RUBELLITE A variety of tourmaline, lithium-aluminium borosilicate	114	Deep pink, brownish pink, to crimson	Transparent	H = 7 G = 3.1	Brazil, Madagascar, California	Brilliant-step cut—sometimes cut as Chinese ornamental pendants
RUBY A variety of corundum, aluminium sesquioxide	90	Brilliant red, with purple tones	Transparent	H = 9 G = 4.03	Burma, Siam, Ceylon, N. Carolina	Brilliant-step cut, step cut
SAPPHIRE A variety of corundum, aluminium sesquioxide	91	Corn-flower blue	Transparent	H = 9 G = 4.03	Kashmir, Ceylon, Australia, Montana	Brilliant, brilliant-step cut
SERPENTINE Hydrous magnesium silicate	167	Yellowish green to gray green	Translucent	H = 2.5 to 4 G = 2.5 to 2.6	Universally distributed	Sometimes carved in ornamental objects
SPESSARTITE A variety of garnet, manganese-aluminium silicate	108	Aurora-red	Transparent to translucent	H = 7 G = 4.2	Ceylon, Virginia	Table cut, brilliant-step cut
SPINEL Magnesium aluminate	105	Fiery red, rose red, violet, blue, green, yellow	Transparent	H = 8 G = 3.5 to 4.1	Burma, Siam, Ceylon	Brilliant, brilliant-step cut, step cut
TOPAZ Aluminium fluo-silicate	102	Sherry yellow to tawny yellow, light blue, white, pink	Transparent	H = 8 G = 3.4 to 3.6	Brazil, Ural Mountains, Saxony, Japan, Mexico, California, Colorado, Utah	Brilliant-step cut
TOURMALINE GEMS Complex aluminiumborosilicate; see also under Indicolite Rubellite	113	Greenish blue to green, and shading to leaf green, brown	Transparent	H = 7 G = 3.1	Brazil, Madagascar, Belgian Congo, Elba, Italy, Maine, Connecticut	Brilliant, brilliant-step cut
TURQUOIS Hydrous alumina copper phosphate	154	Sky blue	Opaque	H = 6 G = 2.84	Sinai Peninsula, Persia, Turkestan, New Mexico	Cabochon
ZIRCON Zirconium silicate; see under Hyacinth Jacinth	116					

Index

	PAGE
African "green garnet"	174
Agalmatolite	167
Agate	145
Alexandrite	123, 125
Almandine	107
Almandine spinel	105
Amatrice	177
Amazon stone	153
Amber	185
Baltic	186
Burmese	187
fluorescent	186
Roumanian	187
insects in	185
Sicilian	186
testing of	186
"Amberoid"	187
American cut brilliant	50
American matrix	177
Amethyst	135
Brazilian	135
Siberian	135
"Oriental"	92
Amir's ruby mine	91
Amulets	16
Anatase	171
Andalusite	171
Andradite	108
Apatite	172
Aquamarine	96
"Arizona rubies"	107
Artificial coloring of quartz	145
Australian diamond fields	72
Australian opal fields	127
Aventurine	143
Axinite	172
Azurite	159
Balas ruby	105
Baltic amber	186
Barnett, Isaacs	71
Bead cut, round	60
Belgian Congo diamond fields	72
Benitoite	172
Bequem, Louis de	29, 44

	PAGE
Beryl gems	94
Beryllonite	173
Black opals	127
Black pearls	182
Bloodstone	147
"Blued" zircon	117, 118
"Blue ground"	70
"Blue John"	168
Bone turquoise	156
Brabant rose cut	57
Brazilian amethyst	153
Brazilian cut brilliant	47, 49
Brazilian diamonds	69
"Brazilian emerald"	114
Burmese amber	187
Cairngorm	136
Calamine	156
"Caliber" cutting	53
California jade	167
Californite	167
"Cape rubies"	107
Carbuncle	107
Card test	10
Carnelian	144
Cassiterite	173
Chalcedony	143
Chatoyancy	124
Chiastrolite	172
Chinese lapidaries	36
Chinese moss agate	146
Chlorastrolite	173
Chloromelanite	166
Chrysoberyl gems	123
Chrysoberyl yellow	124
"Chrysolite"	124
Chrysoprase	144
Cinnamon stone	108
Citrine	136
Cleopatra's emerald mine	94
Combination brilliant-step cut	51
Copal gum	185
Conchiolin	182
Coral	188
Corner facets	27

PAGE

Corundum gems 90
Crocidolite 142
Cross facets 57
Cross rose cut 58
Crown 27
Crystal balls 133
Crystal balls, testing of 134
Culet 27
Cullinan diamond 84
Cultured pearls 183
Cyanite 173
Cylinder seals 16
Cymophane 124

Demantoid 109
Depth of a cut gem 27
Derbyshire spar 168
Double-cut brilliant 46
     refraction 10
     rose cut 58
Diamond "bruting" 30
     crystal form of 73
Diamond fields, Australia 72
          British Guiana 72
          South African 70
          Brazil 69
          Belgian Congo 72
Diamond "floors" 71
     polishing 31
     pipes 70
     sawing 30
     "slitting" 30
     sorter 28
Diamonds, Arkansas 72
     "carbons" in 29
     "close goods" 28
     colors of 73
     grades of 29
     "off color" 29
     value of 78
Dichroite 175
Dichroscope 109, 116
Diopside 173

East Indian lapidaries 32
Emerald 94
     cut 61
Emeralds, Colombian 94
     North Carolina 95

Salzburg 95
"Spanish" 95
English round-cut brilliant............ 47
     square-cut brilliant 46
     star-cut brilliant 46
Enstatite 174
Essonite 108
"Evening emerald" 118
Euclase 174

Facets, names of 27
Fancy sapphires 92
Feldspar gems 151
     aventurine 153
Fersman, Dr. A. E., cited 82
Figure stone 167
Flèches d'amour 141
Fluor 168
Fluorite 168
Formosa coral 188
Fragility of opals 128
French cut brilliant 53

Gallo-Roman beads 20
Garnet, Bohemian 107
Garnet gems 106
Girdle 27
Golconda 68, 77
Golden beryl 96
Great Mogul diamond 82

Harlequin opal 126
Hawk eye 142
Heart-shaped brilliant 55
Heavy liquids 10
Heliotrope 147
Hematite 174
Hessonite 108
Hiddenite 175
Holland rose cut 57
Hope diamond 83
Hungarian cat's eye 142
     opal 126
Hyacinth 108, 117

"Imperial jade" 166
Indicolite 114
Insects in amber 185
Iolite 175

PAGE

Jacinth 108, 116, 117
Jade 163
    Chinese 164
    implements, prehistoric 163
    ancient American 164
    "Maori" 166
    "mutton fat" 166
    Yunnan 166
Jadeite 163
Jamb peg 34
Jargoon 117
Jasper 147
"Job's tears" 119

Kashmiri sapphires 91
Kauri gum 185, 187
Koh-i-nor diamond 78
Kunz, Dr. G. F. 176
Kunzite 175
Kyanite 173

Labradorite 153
"Lapis, Swiss" 145
Lapis lazuli 156
Light dispersion 11
Lithia emerald 175

Main facets 27
Malachite 158
Matrix turquoise 156
Mazarin, Cardinal 56
"Melting snow" jade 166
Mexican fire opal.................... 127
Milky quartz 137
Mocha stone 146
Moonstone 152
Morgan Collection of Gems....xiii, 6
Morganite 96
Morion 137
Moss agate 146
"Mother of emerald" 142

Nacre 182
Necklace, the evolution of the....19-20
    Morocco ceremonial 21
Nephrite 163
Nicolo 146

Odontolite 156

PAGE

Octahedrite 171
Off colored diamonds 29
Old Mine cut brilliant 47-49
Onyx 146
Opal, fire 127
    fossils 127
    gems 126
    source of color 126
"Oriental Amethyst" 92
Oriental cat's eye 123-124
    opals 126
    topaz 92-102
Orloff diamond 81

Pagoda stone 167
"Pavilion" 27
Pearl 181
    "base" 184
    conch 184
    fresh water 184
    grain 184
    "orient" 182
    Oriental 182
Pendant cut brilliant 55
Pendeloque cutting 59
Peridot 118
    Burma 119
    Levantine 119
Persian seal amulets 18-19
Phenacite 176
Picrometer 9
Pitt, Sir Thomas 80
Pitt diamond 80
Prase 142
"Precious and semiprecious" stones
    defined 89
Prehnite 176
Pyrite 176
Pyrope 107

Quartz cat's eye 125, 142

Reflection and refraction in a cut
    gem 26
Regent diamond 80
Rhodes, Cecil 71
Rhodolite 107
Rhodonite 158
"River diggings" 70

	PAGE
Rock crystal	132
Rock crystal balls	133
Rondels	133
Rose cut	56
Rose quartz	137
Rose recoupé	58
Rosette cut	56
Roumanian amber	187
Rubies	91
North Carolina	92
Siamese	91
Ruby	90
"Ruby of the Black Prince"	105
Ruby, "pigeon blood"	90
Rubellite	114
Rubicelle	105
Russian carving in quartz	135
Russian lapis	157
Rutilated quartz	141
Rutile	174
Sagenite	141
Sancy diamond	82
Sardonyx	146
Satin spar	168
Saussurite	167
Sapphire	91
Ceylonese	92
Fancy	5, 92
Montana	92
Star	93
Sapphirine	143
Sard	144
Scarabs, Egyptian	18
Scotch topaz	137
Selenite	168
Serpentine	167
Shell cameo	188
Siberian amethyst	135
lapis	157
Sicilian amber	186
Single cut brilliant	45
"Skill facets"	27
"Slitting" wheels	33
Smithsonite	156
Sodalite	158
Southwest Africa diamond field	72
Spanish topaz	137
Specific gravity	7, 8, 9

	PAGE
Spinel gems	105
ruby	105
Sphalerite	176
Spessartite	108
Sphene	177
"Split facets"	27
"Spread" of a cut gem	27
Square-cut brilliant	45
"Star facets"	27
"Star of Africa"	85
Star rubies	92
sapphires	92
Step cut	61
Stuart Range opal field	128
Sunstone	153
Swiss lapis	145
Synthetic rubies	93
sapphires	93
Syriam garnets	108
"Table"	27
Table cut brilliant	50, 51
Talmudic legend of garnet	107
Tavernier, Jean Baptiste	82, 83
Testing amber	186
Thetis hairstone	142
Thomsonite	177
Tiger eye	142
Titanite	177
Tomb jade	165
Topaz gems	102
"pinked"	103
precious	102
Tourmaline, distribution of color in	115
gems	113
parti-colored	114, 115
Turquoise	154
Turquoise matrix	156
Variscite	177
Venus's hairstone	141
Vesuvianite	178
Water sapphire	175
White Cliffs opals	127
"Yellow ground"	70
Zircon gems	116

A CATALOG OF SELECTED
DOVER BOOKS
IN ALL FIELDS OF INTEREST

A CATALOG OF SELECTED DOVER
BOOKS IN ALL FIELDS OF INTEREST

CONCERNING THE SPIRITUAL IN ART, Wassily Kandinsky. Pioneering work by father of abstract art. Thoughts on color theory, nature of art. Analysis of earlier masters. 12 illustrations. 80pp. of text. 5⅜ x 8½. 23411-8 Pa. $3.95

ANIMALS: 1,419 Copyright-Free Illustrations of Mammals, Birds, Fish, Insects, etc., Jim Harter (ed.). Clear wood engravings present, in extremely lifelike poses, over 1,000 species of animals. One of the most extensive pictorial sourcebooks of its kind. Captions. Index. 284pp. 9 x 12. 23766-4 Pa. $12.95

CELTIC ART: The Methods of Construction, George Bain. Simple geometric techniques for making Celtic interlacements, spirals, Kells-type initials, animals, humans, etc. Over 500 illustrations. 160pp. 9 x 12. (USO) 22923-8 Pa. $9.95

AN ATLAS OF ANATOMY FOR ARTISTS, Fritz Schider. Most thorough reference work on art anatomy in the world. Hundreds of illustrations, including selections from works by Vesalius, Leonardo, Goya, Ingres, Michelangelo, others. 593 illustrations. 192pp. 7⅛ x 10¼. 20241-0 Pa. $9 95

CELTIC HAND STROKE-BY-STROKE (Irish Half-Uncial from "The Book of Kells"): An Arthur Baker Calligraphy Manual, Arthur Baker. Complete guide to creating each letter of the alphabet in distinctive Celtic manner. Covers hand position, strokes, pens, inks, paper, more. Illustrated. 48pp. 8¼ x 11. 24336-2 Pa. $3.95

EASY ORIGAMI, John Montroll. Charming collection of 32 projects (hat, cup, pelican, piano, swan, many more) specially designed for the novice origami hobbyist. Clearly illustrated easy-to-follow instructions insure that even beginning papercrafters will achieve successful results. 48pp. 8¼ x 11. 27298-2 Pa. $2.95

THE COMPLETE BOOK OF BIRDHOUSE CONSTRUCTION FOR WOOD-WORKERS, Scott D. Campbell. Detailed instructions, illustrations, tables. Also data on bird habitat and instinct patterns. Bibliography. 3 tables. 63 illustrations in 15 figures. 48pp. 5¼ x 8½. 24407-5 Pa. $2.50

BLOOMINGDALE'S ILLUSTRATED 1886 CATALOG: Fashions, Dry Goods and Housewares, Bloomingdale Brothers. Famed merchants' extremely rare catalog depicting about 1,700 products: clothing, housewares, firearms, dry goods, jewelry, more. Invaluable for dating, identifying vintage items. Also, copyright-free graphics for artists, designers. Co-published with Henry Ford Museum & Greenfield Village. 160pp. 8¼ x 11. 25780-0 Pa. $9.95

HISTORIC COSTUME IN PICTURES, Braun & Schneider. Over 1,450 costumed figures in clearly detailed engravings–from dawn of civilization to end of 19th century. Captions. Many folk costumes. 256pp. 8⅜ x 11¾. 23150-X Pa. $12.95

THE INFLUENCE OF SEA POWER UPON HISTORY, 1660–1783, A. T. Mahan. Influential classic of naval history and tactics still used as text in war colleges. First paperback edition. 4 maps. 24 battle plans. 640pp. 5⅜ x 8½. 25509-3 Pa. $12.95

THE STORY OF THE TITANIC AS TOLD BY ITS SURVIVORS, Jack Winocour (ed.). What it was really like. Panic, despair, shocking inefficiency, and a little heroism. More thrilling than any fictional account. 26 illustrations. 320pp. 5⅜ x 8½. 20610-6 Pa. $8.95

FAIRY AND FOLK TALES OF THE IRISH PEASANTRY, William Butler Yeats (ed.). Treasury of 64 tales from the twilight world of Celtic myth and legend: "The Soul Cages," "The Kildare Pooka," "King O'Toole and his Goose," many more. Introduction and Notes by W. B. Yeats. 352pp. 5⅜ x 8½. 26941-8 Pa. $8.95

BUDDHIST MAHAYANA TEXTS, E. B. Cowell and Others (eds.). Superb, accurate translations of basic documents in Mahayana Buddhism, highly important in history of religions. The Buddha-karita of Asvaghosha, Larger Sukhavativyuha, more. 448pp. 5⅜ x 8½. 25552-2 Pa. $9.95

ONE TWO THREE . . . INFINITY: Facts and Speculations of Science, George Gamow. Great physicist's fascinating, readable overview of contemporary science: number theory, relativity, fourth dimension, entropy, genes, atomic structure, much more. 128 illustrations. Index. 352pp. 5⅜ x 8½. 25664-2 Pa. $8.95

ENGINEERING IN HISTORY, Richard Shelton Kirby, et al. Broad, nontechnical survey of history's major technological advances: birth of Greek science, industrial revolution, electricity and applied science, 20th-century automation, much more. 181 illustrations. ". . . excellent . . ."–*Isis.* Bibliography. vii + 530pp. 5⅜ x 8¼. 26412-2 Pa. $14.95

DALÍ ON MODERN ART: The Cuckolds of Antiquated Modern Art, Salvador Dalí. Influential painter skewers modern art and its practitioners. Outrageous evaluations of Picasso, Cézanne, Turner, more. 15 renderings of paintings discussed. 44 calligraphic decorations by Dalí. 96pp. 5⅜ x 8½. (USO) 29220-7 Pa. $4.95

ANTIQUE PLAYING CARDS: A Pictorial History, Henry René D'Allemagne. Over 900 elaborate, decorative images from rare playing cards (14th–20th centuries): Bacchus, death, dancing dogs, hunting scenes, royal coats of arms, players cheating, much more. 96pp. 9¼ x 12¼. 29265-7 Pa. $11.95

MAKING FURNITURE MASTERPIECES: 30 Projects with Measured Drawings, Franklin H. Gottshall. Step-by-step instructions, illustrations for constructing handsome, useful pieces, among them a Sheraton desk, Chippendale chair, Spanish desk, Queen Anne table and a William and Mary dressing mirror. 224pp. 8⅛ x 11¼. 29338-6 Pa. $13.95

THE FOSSIL BOOK: A Record of Prehistoric Life, Patricia V. Rich et al. Profusely illustrated definitive guide covers everything from single-celled organisms and dinosaurs to birds and mammals and the interplay between climate and man. Over 1,500 illustrations. 760pp. 7½ x 10⅛. 29371-8 Pa. $29.95

Prices subject to change without notice.

Available at your book dealer or write for free catalog to Dept. GI, Dover Publications, Inc., 31 East 2nd St., Mineola, N.Y. 11501. Dover publishes more than 500 books each year on science, elementary and advanced mathematics, biology, music, art, literary history, social sciences and other areas.